Kisses

From the Father

COMING FACE TO FACE
WITH THE LOVE OF GOD

Michael Flesaker
490 - 7245

Kisses
From the Father

COMING FACE TO FACE WITH THE LOVE OF GOD

by
Dr. Ron Phillips

Harrison House
Tulsa, Oklahoma

06 05 04 03   10 9 8 7 6 5 4 3 2 1

Kisses From the Father—
Coming Face to Face With the Love of God
ISBN 1-57794-577-8
Copyright © 2003 by Dr. Ron Phillips
5208 Hixson Pike
Hixson, TN 37343
www.ronphillips.org

Published by Harrison House, Inc.
P. O. Box 35035
Tulsa, Oklahoma 74153

Like Ron Phillips, I grew up in a dysfunctional home. I can relate to his story and reaffirm that our heavenly Father is here to meet our needs. Those who read *Kisses From the Father* will be reminded of God's deep love for His children and encouraged to pursue an intimate relationship with Him. Having spoken in Ron's church, I know that there is fruit in the lives of his church members and their focus is indeed on the Father.

—*James Robison*
Founder & President
LIFE Outreach International
Fort Worth, Texas

This is your moment for empowerment! *Kisses From the Father* paints a very solid picture of who we *really* are through the unfailing, unmatched love of the Father. Dr. Phillips lays it out plain and simple. Read it, receive it and rejoice in it on your way to Divine Destiny.

—*Bishop Eddie L. Long*
Senior Pastor
New Birth Missionary Baptist Church
Lithonia, GA

The very word revival is usually associated with words such as *power, dynamo—nation-shaking power.* Yet the hallmark of true revival is entering into an intimate relationship with the Father. In his new book, my friend, Dr. Ron Phillips oozes with kisses from the Father.

—*John A. Kilpatrick*
Senior Pastor
Brownsville Assembly of God
Pensacola, Florida

This new work by Dr. Ron Phillips is perhaps his best yet. *Kisses From the Father* reminds us all that we have a heavenly Father who wants to be a loving "daddy" to His children. He is the Father of all fathers. He invites us to sit at His feet, abide in His house, and rest in His arms...and with Him all things are possible. He is Abba Father!

—*Tommy Tenney*
Author, The God Chasers
President & CEO of The GodChasers.network

Contents

Foreword

The greatest thing in the world is the love of a father. Nothing rivals its power to heal, restore, mend, and make all things new. A father's love surpasses all other virtues. Set into our lives like a crown jewel, the love of the Father shimmers in our lives as we are embraced in tender and loving arms.

Ron Philips unveils this hidden treasure to us as we explore the true essence of embracing the love of God face to face. In God's scheme of things, nothing has power over His love. We are loved because it is in God's nature as a Father to love us regardless of what we have done.

Ron has moved in and out of life's difficulties and maintained his allegiance to God with true passion and commitment. His love for the Word of God and his zeal to touch hurting humanity shines through his life.

We are in this walk together as we transform lives, heal hearts, and win souls for the Kingdom of God. This book will fill you with compassion as you recognize the Father as your protector; your faith will be renewed to honor Him as your Father. As you read these pages, God, I'm certain, will smile upon you and hold you tenderly as you experience *Kisses From the Father.*

—*Paula White*
Without Walls International Church
Tampa, Florida

Preface

Nothing makes us feel safer than being curled in the embrace of one's father. Yet Christianity today doesn't explore this idea very deeply. It seems the forgotten member of the Godhead is "the Father." While hundreds of books fill the shelves about our dear Savior, Jesus Christ, and the blessed Holy Spirit, only a few are found on the subject of God as our Father.

I believe the time has come for a clear presentation of the Father. This generation, with a staggering number of children of the free world living in fatherless households, needs this comforting revelation. The four Gospels have hundreds of references to God as Father, yet we seldom hear a sermon on the topic of His Fatherhood to us.

The devil knows that divine power can be released in the individual who finds the acceptance and love of God the Father. In this day of family dysfunction, absent parents, and abusive or indifferent fathers, be assured that there is a Father in heaven who is personally interested in every detail of our lives, who showers blessings from heaven upon us, kissing us with mercy and peace when we most need it. Read on and discover the everlasting embrace of our heavenly Father!

Introduction

It was years ago in the Frankfurt airport on a cold morning. I had been on the plane all night, traveling to Israel, and was trekking the half-mile journey through the crowded terminal to where I hoped my luggage would be waiting.

As was often the case on these tour-group flights to the Holy Land, some passengers were Orthodox Jews traveling home. Among them was one gentleman who stood out from the rest, not so much because he wore the traditional black hat, suit, and ringlet curls with his full beard, but because he had his large family with him.

It was a tangled mess for any parents to find themselves in. Can you imagine 300 to 400 people with their carts and their luggage scurrying in every direction, and you and your family waiting to have every square inch of your luggage searched?

Understandably, the children were restless. One young son, about four years of age, strayed briefly from his daddy in the midst of all the luggage and clutter and turned in fright to search for him.

I can still hear it: "Abba! Abba! Abba! Abba! Abba!" His daddy almost immediately heard his voice and called him, picked him up, and comforted him. He was

saying words in Hebrew and Yiddish that I didn't understand, but I understood "Abba."

Term of Endearment

Abba is an Aramaic word that Hebrew children have used for centuries to convey the affection of "Daddy" or "Papa." It is found three times in the New Testament. One of these was in the Garden of Gethsemane, when Jesus prayed, "...Abba, Father...Take this cup away from Me...."[1] At the most critical moment of His earthly life, this was the title Jesus used for His Father.

In another passage we find that the apostle Paul linked the Christian's cry of "Abba, Father" with the "Spirit of adoption."[2] In yet another Scripture, Paul wrote, "Because you are sons, God has sent forth the Spirit of His Son into your hearts, crying out, 'Abba, Father!'"[3]

The endearing term was common in the mixed dialect of Palestine and was used by children in addressing their father.[4] Servants were not permitted to use this title in addressing the head of the house. In daily usage it really is like a personal name, in contrast to the more formal term "Father," which is always connected to "Abba" in the New Testament. This joining of the two words is probably due to the fact that "Abba" practically had become a proper name, and Greek-speaking Jews added the Greek word *pater,* "father," from the language they used. "Abba" is the word framed by the lips of infants and shows unreasoning trust. According to W.E. Vine in *Expository Dictionary of New Testament Words,* the term "...'father' expresses an intelligent apprehension of the relationship. The two together express the love and intelligent confidence of the child."[5]

Our Cry to Daddy God

As I stood there in the airport that day, God's gentle Spirit washed over me, and I was overwhelmed to know that I had the right to reach up to the God of the universe and call Him "Abba." You see, the right to call God "Abba" belongs to those who have truly received Him into their lives by accepting His Son Jesus as their Lord and Savior, evidenced by the Holy Spirit at work in their heart, affirming their sonship to God.

This cry of "Abba" is said to proceed from the Holy Spirit in us, drawing forth the exclamation in our hearts. The cry explodes from our hearts under the vitalizing energy of the Spirit as the very element of the new life in believers.

The name "Abba" speaks of closeness and tenderness. It makes God more reachable and personal. This title sets forth His real nature and feelings toward His children. He is our "Papa" or "Daddy" God. He is One

who cradles us in His arms and loves us. He is the One who carries us when we are weak. He stands on the porch of His great house and waits for us to come home. He is the Father that many do not have in today's world.

Your life may be lost in the luggage of life. You may look around and see yourself all alone. You may feel like everything has gone wrong. You may have momentarily lost sight of the fact that God loves you. That's why He sent the Holy Spirit—so that you can say, "Abba! Abba! Abba!" He will say, "I'm here! I'm here! I'm here! I'm here to meet your needs."

SECTION ONE

For this reason...I bow my knees [in prayer] before the Father of our Lord Jesus Christ,

For Whom every family in heaven and on earth is named [that Father from Whom all fatherhood takes its title and derives its name].

EPHESIANS 3:14,15 AMP

Chapter 1

Search for the Father

I remember that it was an exceptionally hot day for March. Yet the unusual and difficult had become the norm for 1991. I turned in to the church parking lot, parked my car, and made my way into the office area. Immediately the coolness of air-conditioning seemed to slap me in the face.

As I walked into the secretarial area in front of my office, I noticed several staff members lingering around, talking in low tones. Carolyn, my administrative assistant, moved out from the group and with a tremble in her voice said, "You need to call your sister-in-law."

I walked quickly into my office, filled suddenly with anxiety and wondering why Sandy would be contacting me. I sat down at my desk, pushed aside the stacks of notes and other evidence of work waiting to be done, dialed the number, and waited.

As Sandy answered, she cut right to the chase and said gently, "Ronnie, R.P. is gone." R.P. was the nickname given to my dad by all my father's friends.

Not comprehending her words, I replied, "Gone where?"

"Gone to heaven," she said.

In that instant, I suddenly felt as if I was moving through time. Tears and memories began to flood my consciousness. Daddy was gone! This man who had once been a stranger, but later a father and a friend, had now departed my life.

I remember at first thinking that this news was impossible. After all, I had just spoken to him by phone the evening before.

"Son," he had asked, "how were services? Did you have any aisle traffic?"

I had chuckled at his question, his way of asking if anyone had made decisions for Christ. I reported on the services and asked about Mother and about the church where he served as deacon.

"Well, Mother isn't doing well," Dad had said. "But I went on to Sunday school and worship by myself. Then this afternoon I called on our visitors from the morning service, and after that I went back for discipleship training and evening worship."

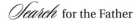

I teared up at the memory of his words—Dad had spent his last full day on earth serving the Lord! Sitting there at my desk in an emotional haze, I phoned my wife, Paulette, and she began gathering our three children. My staff quickly and calmly helped me gather myself and leave the office. At home, our family packed the car and started the four-hour ride to Montgomery, Alabama.

As the miles passed, the children talked as if their granddaddy were still alive. Kelli, Heather, and Ronnie Jr. began to reminisce about all of the ice cream, candy, and treats they enjoyed with Granddad. My mind was in complete denial. *He can't be dead,* I thought. *I have so much to tell him, and there is so much I want to know about him.*

While the children talked and Paulette drove, I drifted off into a semi-sleep. Again I felt I was skipping back and forth in time.

I remembered first that he was a man I had once feared and disliked. Dad was a weekend alcoholic for many years. He would work hard all week and then on Friday he would start drinking, concluding the drinking binge on Saturday night. My dear mother would try to stop him, and loud fights ensued. I can remember hiding under the bed until the noise ceased.

Christmas was especially a bad time. Mother worked at a department store and would try so hard to

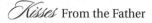

have everything nice. Inevitably on Christmas Eve, Dad would stagger in drunk, and an evening that should have been joyful family time would be reduced to tears and fears.

I remembered the ball games Dad did not attend. I had been a starter on the junior high football team. During one game I recall making an amazing tackle to stop the opposing team, only to turn and realize that no one that mattered even saw it. I remembered walking home over two miles from school after practicing in the dark alone. I was motivated to achieve so that some man, any man would say, "You did good, boy—I am proud of you."

I remembered one fearful evening when I was fourteen. I was angry about the drunkenness, waste, and abuse that engulfed our family. I had grown to be large for my age, so I decided to stand up to Daddy. He came in drinking, and immediately the fight was on with Mother. He threatened her, and I stepped between them fully prepared to hit my daddy with my fist. Before I could react, he acted, smashing a glass bowl over my head. He ran me out of our modest little house saying, "Don't ever come back."

I had never felt more alone and forsaken in my life. I fled in pain and tears. A slight cut caused blood to run down my face and mix with the tears of grief. Where would I go? What would I do? I felt the pain of over a

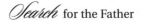

decade of abuse and absenteeism by my father flood over me. I wanted to die! I walked out onto a railroad trestle with suicidal thoughts. I sat on the trestle, waiting for a train to run over me or for the courage to jump into the flooding creek below.

God used that situation to reach out to me, for on that trestle, Abba Father spoke to me in my heart and promised me help. As I detailed in the book *The Spirit of Christmas*,[1] I experienced His abundant strength, and this event proved to be the turning point in my dad's life.

Changed by God's Love

I snapped out of my reverie to discover that we were less than an hour away from Montgomery. Looking in the backseat, I saw my kids now dozing. I smiled as I watched their peaceful faces and thought how thankful I was that my kids had never seen Granddaddy drunk or abusive.

Shortly after the violent incident of my fourteenth year, Dad came back to the Lord. By then, I had given my life to the ministry, and soon he began to take an interest in me. It was late, but not too late, when he timidly showed up in my life. He drove me to some of my first preaching assignments. I remember how proud he was at my wedding, and later, at my three

graduations. He loved on his grandchildren and showered them with tokens of his affection.

We loved each other more as the years went by, but we never talked about the past. We needed to and we planned to, but we didn't. At age fifty-nine Dad was ordained a deacon. I preached the service and wept as I laid my hands upon his balding head.

I retreated back from these thoughts of long ago as we pulled into the driveway of Mom and Dad's home. It was overwhelming to walk into the house and see his recliner sitting empty. I embraced my mother, brother, and sisters, and we wept for a long while. There was much to do and agree upon about the funeral and about Mother's needs. My brother, Rupert, very efficiently took care of most of the details.

Dad's car was sitting under the portico. I went out and sat in it for a few moments. I could smell his cologne still lingering in the air and upholstery. I turned the car on and immediately heard a tape playing—the SonLife Quartet from our church. It was probably the last music he heard on earth. I missed him already.

His absence in my early years wounded me, and his presence in my later years had begun to heal me. Yet I felt cheated and robbed now that he had gone so quickly.

The funeral service was packed, and I met so many people Daddy had befriended or won to Christ. Though I had made great strides in the past fifteen

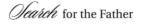

years in getting to know him, I realized I did not really know him in depth. But it was too late to talk to him. He was gone!

However, the funeral and days following gave me the opportunity to find out about Dad through those who had known him all his life. I learned that his mother, Mary, had died when he was very young. Because Dad's father was an absent parent, unable to care for the children, they were all placed in homes of relatives.

I thought of my father's childhood as I recently read a very popular children's book in preparation for a radio series on the topic of children and media. I was amazed to read that the author had created an environment for the main character much like what my father experienced. From relatives, I learned that Dad had lived in a closet at the home of his aunt and uncle who had two children of their own.

In those sad years, he knew a great amount of neglect. I discovered that the aunt and uncle would often buy ice cream for their children and not give any to Dad. One day his uncle promised to take them all to the county fair if certain tasks were completed. Daddy worked hard and even helped the other children complete their chores. But in the end, the aunt would not allow Dad to go. This crushed him and added to his pain and grief.

I learned that by age fourteen Dad was on his own, living with strangers and running moonshine whiskey. Dad had lived in poverty, loneliness, and neglect. He had scratched out a living in the underworld of the "redneck Mafia" of Alabama.

But World War II saved him from a lifetime of crime and changed his life. He joined the Air Force, and the rigors of war and the discipline of military life began to change Dad. He received a Purple Heart and other medals for valor.

He received his GED diploma after the war and took a job in the insurance business. He worked for the same company all his life. However, the hurt and the pain of his own childhood stayed with him and precipitated his drinking problem.

I was the third generation affected by poor fathering. My dad was in pain and fought the early rejection all of his life. I became a victim of his pain and suffered for years, until the day he was changed by the power of God's love.

Finding a Family

Why do I tell you this deeply personal story? So you will know that I understand the absentee father and the abusive father. Much of the family tragedy we face today is due to failure of fathers. I applaud every effort

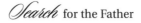

to teach and strengthen men to assume their roles, and that task must continue. However, the problems I had were not solved because my dad became perfect. I was able to grow and thrive in life because I discovered that I had a heavenly Father who was watching over me!

Jesus Christ came not only to save us from hell later, but also to bring us into a family now. He came to let us all know that we have a heavenly Father who desires to love us and lead us!

When I felt total despair and did not want to live, my heavenly Father showed up to rescue me. Perhaps you are at that same place. Maybe you have never felt totally safe. It could be that you doubt the trustworthiness of God as your Father. Maybe you long for a closer relationship with Him but feel walls of guilt and distance separating you from that intimacy with Daddy God.

I am writing this book so you can experience a revelation of your heavenly Father. I want you to know more than the theology of God the Father—I want you to experience His great arms around you.

For many years I lived in fear of my earthly father because I did not know him. What I saw of him in my early days was not who he really was, but rather a marred image. When he allowed God to change him, I discovered that he had always loved me.

This attitude affects our understanding of our heavenly Father. Because we don't know Him, we fear Him. We also tend to blame Him for the difficulties we face.

Today, thousands of children live with similar pain. It is sobering to read reports such as the *2001 National Journal* article that states, "...by some estimates, 60 percent of all American children born in the 1990s will spend some significant portion of their childhood in a fatherless home."[2] Other children live in abuse and neglect. God knows that there are no perfect families. Yet we have a perfect Father in God!

You see, the Father, our Abba, knew the dysfunctional situations many of us would be reared in. He knew the pain and the wounds some of us would carry. Even those who have been blessed with healthy, happy family relationships sometimes still struggle with relating to God as their Father. But God knew we would struggle, so His Son Jesus came to bring us face to face and heart to heart with our Father in heaven. In the chapters to follow, we will discover the deep love He has for us all.

Chapter Two

The *Forever* Father

I couldn't help notice the young girl standing quietly weeping on the other side of the altar. Everything about her seemed to cry out for help.

God had moved powerfully in the revival service that had just concluded. I had spoken a strong word about forgiving those who had caused hurt to one's life. A long line of weeping people stood waiting at the altar for prayer, and I began praying over them one by one. Many we ministered to in that line found freedom and peace as they released past hurts into God's care.

When I finally stepped in front of the girl, I noticed that the pain in her eyes and the drawn look on her face made her look older than her thirteen years. Speaking brokenly at first and then letting the painful words tumble out in a rush, she told me that she was a resident in a home for addicted teens. She had turned to drugs as an escape from an abusive home. Her father had sexually molested her beginning at age nine. When

the girl had tried to reveal it to her mother, the mother had slapped her daughter, calling her a liar.

This young girl had stayed in her home until she was eleven and then hit the streets, losing herself in the drug culture. Over time, her life moved into a more vicious cycle of drugs and abuse.

She told me how juvenile authorities had found her and placed her into the Christian center where she now lived. Looking up at me in tears she said, "I am clean from drugs but not from pain. I have no father or mother anymore. No one really loves me. Sometimes I want to die."

How my heart wrenched as I heard her sorrowful words. The Holy Spirit rose up in me, and as I looked into those tired, lonely eyes, I spoke clearly and gently, "You have a forever Father, and a big Brother, and a faithful family!"

Taking her aside, I told her the story of Jesus being abused and nailed to the cross. I explained how His suffering paid an awful price to rescue us all. I then told her about how we could each know our Abba Father, using the story of the Prodigal Son in Luke 15 as an example.

I told her that God wanted her to be His daughter and that He would never leave her or hurt her. She collapsed, weeping, and asked Him into her life. I knew that there was rejoicing in heaven over this new daughter!

Just recently I received a brief e-mail message from her, and she is recovering and growing in the Lord.

Children of an Everlasting Father

My young friend discovered what the great preacher Charles Hadden Spurgeon wrote about the Father's love:

> "...*Father!*—Here is a kingly attribute so sweetly veiled in love, that the King's crown is forgotten in the King's face, and His scepter becomes, not a rod of iron, but a silver scepter of mercy—the scepter indeed seems to be forgotten in the tender hand of Him who wields it. Father!—Here is honour and love. How great is a Father's love to his children! That which friendship cannot do, and mere benevolence will not attempt, a father's heart and hand must do for his sons. They are his offspring, he must bless them; they are his children, he must show himself strong in their defense. If an earthly father watches over his children with unceasing love and care, how much more does our heavenly Father? Abba, Father! He who can say this, hath uttered better music than cherubim or seraphim can reach. There is heaven in the depth of that word—Father! There is all I can ask; all my necessities can demand; all my wishes can desire. I have all in all to all eternity when I can say, Father."[1]

The young woman I described, like so many of this generation, was reared without a father's true love. Many thousands of others are living with single mothers, the fathers absent.

God, our Father, did not create sons and daughters to cause them pain. We were created for His pleasure and glory. On the first pages of Scripture, we may find a hint as to why God wanted children.

> *"...It is not good that man should be alone...."*
>
> Genesis 2:18

God may not have "needed" us, as some theologians state, but I believe that He truly wanted us. I believe the Father God wanted a large family in order to demonstrate His love. He created Adam and Eve and lavished His love upon them. When Adam failed, plunging humanity into sin, our Father purposed to send a second Son, begotten of a virgin, into the world to bring His family home.

Even those who have refused to come home are not called vile names by the seeking Father. They are simply referred to as "lost." They are children who need to be found and brought home.

Finding His Children

When my daughter Heather was in high school, she gave me a terrible fright. On a youth outing to a wilderness state park, she and her friend stepped off a trail to see a scenic view. The two girls lost their way.

Waiting at the church with the other parents, I watched the vehicles pull up and was stunned when my daughter did not emerge. The youth director had chosen to return to the church without the girls. Understandably angry, I confronted the director, saying, "You left my daughter up there lost? Why didn't you or another leader stay?" I was rushing out the door, intending to make the 70-mile drive back to the park myself, when the authorities called to say they had found the girls safe.

The idea of my child being lost shook me as no other event ever had. I was relieved to know she was now safe but still felt anger that no leader from the group had stayed behind until she was found. The youth pastor's comment to me told the story, for he said, "I felt I needed to stay with the group. For after all, Pastor, she is not my daughter."

He was right about one thing: He did not know my heart as her father. Knowing how strongly I felt at the moment that my child was lost, I can imagine how Abba must feel with countless millions of His children still floundering in loneliness and sin, without a Savior! We know He cared enough to come Himself to find us. The prophets promised His coming:

For unto us a Child is born, unto us a Son is given; and the government will be upon His shoulder. And His name will be called wonderful, Counselor, Mighty God, everlasting Father, Prince of Peace.

Isaiah 9:6

Jesus proclaimed Himself as the fulfillment of that promise when He said, "For the Son of Man has come to seek and to save that which was lost."[2]

Abba's Eternal Provision

Abba knew we would have dysfunctional families. He knew that we needed an "everlasting Father," that we needed a Daddy who wouldn't abuse or abandon us.

While Jesus was on earth, our Abba was here in person. He said, "...He who has seen Me has seen the Father...."[3]

When it was time for Him to go back to heaven, He told His grieving friends, "I will not leave you orphans...."[4]

You see, just prior to that He had promised to send the Holy Spirit, who is God the Father in us.[5] That is why I believe the primary evidence of the Spirit's coming into our lives is being able to cry "Abba Father."

Long before spiritual gifts and graces are understood, the new believer needs the embrace of Abba. We need to learn to receive His love and care. No wonder the original Greek word for worship, *proskuneo*, means "first kiss" or "to kiss toward."[6] The father of the Prodigal Son covered his face with kisses upon the son's return.[7] Worship is when we learn to kiss our Abba back!

God enjoys being a Father! When God sent Moses to deliver Israel from the slavery of Egypt, God told him to remind Pharaoh: "...Israel is My son, My firstborn."[8]

In our language, God was saying to Pharaoh, "Don't mess with My children...."

Later, David, whose earthly father didn't highly regard him[9] and whose "father-figure," Saul, abused him,[10] made this confession about God as Father: "As a father pities his children, so the Lord pities those who fear Him."[11]

Isaiah would sound out his own heart cry: "Doubtless You are our Father, though Abraham was ignorant of us, and Israel does not acknowledge us. You, O Lord, are our Father; our Redeemer from Everlasting is Your name."[12]

The curtain would fall on the Old Testament with Malachi's plaintive appeal: "Have we not all one Father? Has not one God created us? Why do we deal treacherously with one another by profaning the covenant of the fathers?"[13]

Father of All Fathers

God the Father showed up in the skin of His Son Jesus of Nazareth. He came to raise up a new race, a

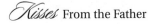

new family, as we read in Ephesians 3:14-15: "For this reason I bow my knees to the Father of our Lord Jesus Christ, from whom the whole family in heaven and earth is named." This phrase "whole family" could be translated "all fatherhood..." (as *The Amplified Bible* says). God is the Daddy of all daddies! In fact, Scripture ascribes Fatherhood to Him in many ways. I can rejoice over each of these aspects of my Father.

I am glad He is Father of the angels.[14]

I celebrate that He is Father of lights.[15]

I am grateful that He is Father of spirits.[16]

Let all of religion know that there is One Father![17]

But I am more excited that my God is "Daddy of all daddies." What a comfort to us that He can find the lost, like the young lady I met (whom we saw earlier), who have never known a true and powerful love, especially from their fathers. God has an unlimited supply of love and a warm embrace for all who need Him.

On a day you feel you are floundering in this life, unsure of your way, be confident and turn to Him. Abba waits for your return on the front porch of eternity.

Chapter 3

Abba Story:
Kidnapped in Eden

Afternoon had come, and the children awaited with gladness the daily visit of their Father.[1] He had been so good to them. His voice reminded them of the cascading water of the river that flowed through their garden. He knew so much, and upon every visit they showered Him with questions. He took them all in His stride, instructing them about this world He had made for them. Everything was new and exciting to the children here in the beautiful Garden of Eden.

One can only imagine the scene, the surroundings, the beauty, and the harmony and perfect union that Adam and Eve had with their Daddy.

How often they must have strolled through the woods together and watched as even the animals responded to Him with delight. The butterflies danced

at His approach, and the birds sang forth their most elegant symphonies of song.

One evening, their Daddy took them farther into their garden, and together they explored a rushing river. Leaning over the water's edge, their Father fished out a sparkling nugget from the riverbank. He said, "This is gold; you will find it a useful and precious metal!" He went on to show them many wonderful stones and gems, and they exclaimed at each new discovery, but the love in His eyes always stirred their hearts more than the sights they saw.

"What new treasures will we see tonight?" they would ask each other. They knew that when the beautiful blue skies would turn black and the sun would drop for another day, their Father would end the lesson on botany, zoology, or geology, and point to the sky above where millions of stars sparkled brightly. He would speak of the great distance of these far-off bodies of light and how He had placed them all with His hand.

Every night, their Daddy would remind them to nurture their love. The children would smile at each other, and the young woman would touch the side of the young man, both of them remembering how their Father had fashioned her from a rib taken from the young man's side. He often expressed to the Father how grateful he was for his beautiful companion, his soul mate. The Father had seen his loneliness, and now they had each other to love forever.

The children didn't think a deeper happiness could have been possible. There was nothing their hearts desired. They had a loving, protective Father, a perfect environment, and a deep love. There was so much bounty in the garden that they almost never thought about the one thing that was off limits—an obscure little tree that the Father had once pointed out. He had told them not to eat of the fruit, that He knew what was best for them, and they took Him at His word—until another voice spoke to them.

The young woman caught sight of the beautiful creature as she strolled alone one day. His appearance was breathtaking and his voice melodious; not quite like Daddy's voice, but the creature made the young woman instantly at ease.

"Does your Father really have your best interests in mind?" he inquired. The creature seemed astounded that the young woman wasn't allowed to eat the fruit of the unique tree. "Why would your loving Father limit your freedom that way?"

The woman thought about it and was confused in her spirit. *True,* she thought, *why should we be denied anything? The creature said this fruit will make us as wise as our Daddy! I could know all He knows!*

She had already taken steps toward the tree, and grasping the firm fruit in her hand, she took a bite. Then she brought a piece to the young man, and he didn't want to be left out, so he ate along with her.

With that simple feast of fruit, their world came apart.

Evening came, their favorite time with their Daddy. But all they wanted to do was hide. The children and their innocence had been kidnapped by a stranger, and they felt exposed and unsafe for the first time. The glory of their Father that had once clothed them was gone.

"Where are you?" came the sweet voice of their Daddy. But somehow by the timbre of His voice, they sensed He already knew. A deep pain echoed in His resounding question. Love called them to account for their deeds.

Hesitantly they came out from hiding, trying desperately to hide their shame. Their attempts to shift the blame were useless. Soon the verdict was determined for the kidnapper, whose voice they had valued over the words of their Father. They saw the stranger for who he was—a slithering serpent who lusted for power.

But the verdict would not end with condemnation for the serpent; the children also had to face the consequence of their disobedience. They would have to leave their beautiful garden and live in a cursed world governed by the kidnapper. The title deed of what was theirs was taken away. And worst of all, their evening walks with the Father would cease.

In the anguish of this awful season, their Daddy looked upon them with eyes filled with mercy. "I want to take care of you," He said with sadness. He took innocent animals and killed them before His children. They were shocked to witness the cries of agony and crimson blood spilled before their eyes, a sight new to them. They didn't understand at first, until He brought the prepared skins of the animals and covered their bodies so their shame would be hidden. Their grief was complete, for they now understood their actions had brought death.

Then the Father spoke words of hope as they prepared to leave the garden. "I won't leave you forever," He said. "I will send One to rescue you from eternal separation from Me." With these words, the Father left.

The silence was deafening, as they realized the Father's voice could no longer be heard.

His Presence was gone.

And a new, cold world lay before the children. In the stillness, they heard again the cunning voice of the kidnapper. The children shuddered. That first night, they huddled alone under a sky that seemed darker than it ever had before. Their only comfort was the echo of their Daddy's words of hope...*I won't leave you forever.*

Who Is Your Father?

As we see in this heartrending narrative, our enemy, the devil, is a kidnapper. He came after God's kids and stole them. Perhaps there was a cosmic jealousy in this former son of light.[2] Lucifer had been the angel of divine worship. He had lived in the fire of God's Presence. Was he not the favored one of all the hosts of heaven?

Pride brought down the "lightbearer," and he was cast out of heaven.[3] Now he placed himself as the prince of darkness. Because he has always lacked the ability to attack the Father directly, he attacks the object of the Father's love, His children. He vies for the loyalty and love of humanity. Satan placed himself as the substitute father, but he is a father of lies.[4]

For this reason, Jesus came.

The Prince of Peace came and rescued us from the snare that Adam and Eve fell into. Through the cross, He became an eternal sacrifice to all who would receive the unfathomable treasure of the Father's love.

SECTION TWO

The *Pattern* of the *Father*

———◆———

Chapter 4

When You *Hear* Abba's Heart—Abraham

Perhaps you've seen this quaint old saying hanging in a grandmother's house. I have seen it as a beautiful needlework art piece displayed in a hallway:

> "You are nearer to God's heart in a garden
> Than any place else on earth!"

Humankind's craving for a deeper walk and closer embrace with Father God is evident in this little quote. Knowing our needs as He does, our Abba Father provided His Word to guide us into close fellowship with Him.

Pictures of Abba

If you open up the Bible first to the Old Testament and scan briefly over the content, you may think the heartbeat of God as a Father isn't to be found. However,

even though you don't find many direct references to God as Father there, we must remember the Old Testament is a progressive revelation—that much of what we see in *writing* in the New Testament we see in *picture,* or *symbol,* in the Old Testament. Scholars call this "typology," and it is one of the unique ways God chose to communicate truth to us.

Four men are held up in the Old Testament as unique fathers. They are better known by the term *patriarch.* Patriarch simply means "father," just as matriarch means "mother." Some societies were patriarchal, father-led; some were matriarchal, mother-led. God chose for His chosen people the governing of the nations by a patriarchy, a culture to be led by a father leader. That's why God said to Abraham, the first of the great patriarchs, "...in you all the families of the earth shall be blessed."[1]

Some would argue here, "But Abraham is not my father." I must point out that on more than one occasion in the New Testament, Abraham is called the father of us all, the father of everyone who has ever put their faith in Jesus Christ.[2]

What can we learn about our Abba Father through the life of Abraham, the first of the four great patriarchs?

Hearing God's Heart

God wants to build up strength for earthly fathers, whether that fatherhood is over a fleshly family or over an extended family. God Almighty can release power in many areas of your life. God's heart leaned toward Abraham in this same way, and Abraham's life reflected God's heart in four areas: glory, journey, stability, and destiny.

Glory

God first spoke to Abraham when his name was still Abram, and he was living in Ur of the Chaldees. In Genesis 12:1 the Lord said to Abram, "...*Get out of your country*...." I believe that God simply spoke aloud to him. Abram had no Bible, no teacher, no preacher with a prophetic word. We don't have any record of anything but direct revelation.

The New Testament confirms this direct revelation, for in Acts 7:2 where Stephen is about to be stoned to death, we read, "The God of glory appeared to our father Abraham when he was in Mesopotamia...." Stephen recognized the fact that Abraham had a revelation by the very Presence of God—the Lord of glory, or the overwhelming, *crushing majesty* of God.[3]

It was no doubt a huge step for Abraham to leave his city. Historical records show that Ur of Chaldees was a modern city, boasting even indoor plumbing. Ur was a magnificent place of wealth. It would take a huge spiritual encounter to make a man willing to leave such a

place of prosperity and turn to a nomadic life in a tent! It would surely take much more than just a "feeling" in the pit of his stomach to drive a man to uproot everything he's ever known.

What happened to Abraham? I believe the weight of the glory of God was so heavy upon him that he couldn't say no! He couldn't even stop to question what was going to happen or what the outcome would be. When God approached him, Abraham was enveloped in God's glory, and his obedience was the only logical response under such glorious majesty.

Comfort in Heartbeat

Don Osgood wrote a book entitled *Fatherbond* in 1989.[4] He wrote it out of a deeply personal heart experience. In the space of one month, Osgood's father died and his thirteen-year-old son died. And he counts his whole life between the sandwich of those experiences. He let go of his father's hand; then he let go of his son's hand.

Osgood tells how one night in the middle of his deathbed vigil, he was reaching out to lay hands upon his dying thirteen-year-old son. He suddenly and fully felt the glory of God encircle him, completely surround him, and then extend to rest upon the boy. Osgood said that in those three months his son was ill, and especially in the last days of that boy's life, he had an overwhelming sense of a father's heart. Osgood learned that the greatest thing he could leave or give his child was not wealth or even his name or his business. The greatest thing he could do was to impart the crushing majesty of the glory of God to his child.

Part of the ministry of Abba God is to bring the crushing majesty of His Presence upon us all, to overwhelm us with who He is and the role of the father in the home, in spite of our weaknesses and failures. There is a blessing of God's Presence that ought to come out of us to our children, to our children of the flesh and to our children in the spirit. That includes those in pastoral leadership of the church; they ought to be people who have a father's heart toward the body.

Journey

Abraham was a father long before he had even one child! God said, "I'm going to make you a father," and when God spoke it, it was done. But God had to move Abraham to bring the promise to pass.

We have an Abba Father who is always on the move. God is going someplace! When God agreed to give the great leader Moses a glimpse of His glory, He set him in the crevice of a rock and said, "You'll see only my back as I'm moving past."[5]

A loving father will include his children as a part of the journey. Too many fathers are waiting for the opportunity to "really live," saying, "If I can just get my dream house, if I can just retire, if I can just get this or that, then I'm going to really start to live." How much better to grab life by its tail now, and enjoy the journey with your children!

Abraham was on a journey initiated by God, and he threw himself into it wholeheartedly. No doubt his family and his servants all caught his sense of adventure as they learned to pick up their tents day after day and follow the will of God wherever it would lead them.

Fathers in this century often work out that spirit of adventure through family vacations, sometimes with interesting results. I fondly remember some disastrous vacations, for it seems even when things go wrong, you build some amazing memories. On one particularly memorable trip, we were maneuvering through the backside of the desert in Arizona. We'd already had a flat tire and had to fix it. I decided to drive across a peak called Devil's Backbone (the name alone should have raised a red flag). I thought it would be fun going across this mountain and visiting the Dinosaur National Monument where I'd no doubt get into an argument with evolutionists, which besides being interesting fun would also embarrass my kids! I could rival the antics of Griswald, the character played by actor Chevy Chase, in the popular "Vacation" movies any day!

I had no idea that Devil's Backbone was at an altitude of nearly 7,000 feet. I didn't know the road up was only two narrow lanes with no signs. I forgot I had three kids in the backseat who in tense circumstances clearly took it out on one another.

"He's on my side!"

"No, I put this right here!"

"He's not supposed to cross this."

"That's mine—give it back!"

"I'm tired of sitting in the middle."

"I want a window," and on and on.

And here I am, driving a narrow road at 7,000 feet and being the "perfect" example of a calm father: "Shut up! Be quiet! Stop that!" Somehow, though, the sense of adventure carried us through!

Can you imagine Abraham with his large assembly of family and servants in a similar kind of situation?

"Where are we going?"

"I don't know."

"Where are we now?"

"I don't know!"

"How much farther?"

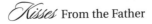

"I don't know!"

Abram's family and servants had to have great trust in their leader, as well as a deep faith in the God who was leading them, to help them retain their spirit of adventure. As a Christian, you must never lose the God-given sense of journey and adventure, either. God wants you to have that. Where would we be in today's modern world if God hadn't poured that spirit of discovery into great men and women?

—Christopher Columbus set sail, certain that a new world awaited his adventurous spirit.

—Johann Sebastian Bach wrote and rewrote music week after week to present fresh worship music to the church.

—Marie Curie brought to mankind the great discovery of artificial radioactivity and the miracle of the X-ray.

—The Wright brothers didn't listen to those who said their attempts at air flight were laughable and a waste of time.

What a challenge and a blessing for us to tell our children, "Look, life is an adventure! God has a special road for you—there's something God wants you to be. Journey on!"

Such was the call of Abraham the patriarch. God gave him a journey that would bring His blessings to countless people. All he had to do was journey on in life on the road of the Father.

Stability

Yet another phase of Abraham's life captures our interest as we read of God's promise to give him a child in his old age. At first, Abraham and Sarah tried to help God's promise along. It had been some time since God had first given him the promise of a son. So Sarah told Abraham to take her young servant girl Hagar and produce a child from her.[6] He did, and Ishmael was born.[7] Although Ishmael became a great nation as God prophesied,[8] he was not the promised seed. The struggle in the Middle East that exists yet today began when Abraham chose to take matters in his own hands.

But when Abraham was 100 years old and Sarah only a few years behind him, he realized God was serious about His promise to them. In Romans 4:19 we read, "And not being weak in faith, he did not consider his own body, already dead (since he was about a hundred years old), and the deadness of Sarah's womb."

Verse 20 goes on to say that Abraham did not waver; he wasn't knocked off balance. He wasn't shaken up. He had lived long enough, seen enough, been on the

journey enough, felt the glory enough that he knew that God could do what He wanted to do. No doubt people would ask, "Abraham, 'father of many nations,' where's your son?" He likely took a breath and replied in faith, "God is going to give me one."

When your life seems to be going crazy, stand firm. Believe God for the impossible. Don't give up. It may hurt in the pit of your stomach where nobody else can feel. Don't let anybody trivialize that pain. But if it's something God promised you, and it looks like it's never going to happen, stand in faith.

Isaac wasn't born of a virgin; God didn't just wave His hand. No, God made Abraham and Sarah as though they were young again! In fact, it wasn't a one-time touch of youth from God. After Sarah died, Abraham took Keturah for his wife and had six more children![9]

God is able!

You can imagine that every time the blessed parents (Abraham and Sarah) looked at Isaac running and growing up before them, they had to have poked each other and laughed and said, "To think we ever doubted!"

Your dream may be dead, the womb of promise may seem dried up, your heart may be broken, you may be at the end of your rope, but don't waver, don't quit, don't stop giving, and don't stop confessing! Go onward!

Destiny

Abraham's destiny was in Isaac. But God wasn't through. In Genesis 22, we read that God tested Abraham. And He said, "Take now your son, your only son...." The Hebrew phrase "your son" could be translated "your beloved son" or "your darling son."[10] A long-awaited child quickly becomes the apple of a parent's eye.

Who can resist the sweetness of a little boy, crawling up into a parent's lap? That father instinct, that mother instinct, causes you to shower him with endearing names, like honey, sweetie, sugar, and so on. It was the same in the Hebrew culture. That's essentially what God said to Abraham. "Take your darling, the apple of your eye, the son of promise, and go to Moriah and offer him there to Me as a sacrifice."

Genesis 22:5 describes Abraham's charge to the rest of his party, "...Stay here with the donkey; the lad and I will go yonder and worship, and we will come back to you." The significance of this statement is explained in Hebrews 11:17-18: "By faith Abraham, when he was tested, offered up Isaac, and he who had received the promises offered up his only begotten son, of whom it was said, 'In Isaac your seed shall be called.'" Abraham was concluding that God wouldn't back down on His promise, even if it meant raising Isaac from the dead to fulfill it.

Abraham put the wood on the boy's back, and they started up that mountain. Soon the haunting question came from young Isaac as he helped his daddy: "Abba, here's the wood; where is the sacrifice?"

And Abraham said, "God will provide."

I believe that pastor and author Arthur Pink was right when he translated that God will provide "Himself" as a sacrifice.[11] That is what the Hebrew would say.[12] Abraham tied his boy to the wood, had the fire of wrath in one hand and the knife of sacrifice in the other. It is hard to imagine his thoughts, for surely his fear and faith mixed together. "In Isaac, my seed was promised, and there's going to come forth children and grandchildren. But God asked me to sacrifice him, so God's going to have to raise him out of the ashes if necessary."

I believe this is why he told the servants, "I and the lad are going to worship, and we will return." Abraham believed there was destiny on this. The destiny of the world and the destiny of a nation awaited the obedience of this man.

You say, "Why did God require that of him?" John 8:56 records the words of Jesus: "Your father Abraham rejoiced to see My day, and he saw it and was glad." On Mount Moriah God showed Himself to Abraham as an Abba Father who provides. Years later, another Son would come! We see Him with wood on His back, going up a mountain, and He too was the darling of His Father's heart, a Father who says, "This is My beloved Son, in whom I am well pleased."[13] Here was a Child who never disobeyed, who always did the will of His Father. But this time, though there were legions of angels at His disposal, the sacrifice proceeded. As Zechariah 13:7 says, "Awake, O sword, against My shepherd..." and into the heart of Jesus the knife of wrath was plunged.

Why did Abraham have to go through this painful test with his son? I believe it stood as a picture of when the Son of the Almighty God would be sacrificed for you and for me. Because of Jesus, we can stand here in the twenty-first century, look each other in the eye, and say with confidence, "For God so loved the world that He gave His only begotten Son, that whoever believes in Him should not perish but have everlasting life."[14]

And as Abba's child, everything you suffer has destiny in it, if you will wait and not waver from His promise. For Abba's heart beats for you, His precious child.

Chapter 5

When Abba
Smiled—Isaac

God has a sense of humor. Everywhere we look, we find examples of that! God created some of the most hilarious creatures in this world of ours.

I personally believe the dog is one of those! Dog lovers may take offense, and I know there are pets that serve useful purposes, but many of them spend their days knocking out your screen doors, digging holes in the yard, and providing you with the means to begin your own fertilizer factory!

Other animals in God's world are just funny to look at. Think about the duckbill platypus or the long-legged ostrich or the prickly porcupine. I believe God had a smile on His face when He put these unique creatures in our world.

Too many of us are far sadder and more mournful than we need to be. Things are a lot better than you think they are. They could be a lot worse than you think they are.

I have heard joy described as the banner flown from the heart when the King is in residence. When talking about our belief in Christ, Simon Peter wrote, "...joy inexpressible and full of glory."[1] And Nehemiah said, "...the joy of the Lord is your strength."[2]

Too many of us are settling with an Ishmael when we should wait for an Isaac. Like Abraham, we are trying to fulfill in the flesh what can only be made complete in the Spirit. Abraham said to God, "Oh, that Ishmael might live before You!" But God said, "...No, Sarah your wife shall bear you a son, and you shall call his name Isaac [laughter]; I will establish My covenant with him for an everlasting covenant, and with his descendents after him."[3]

Galatians 4:6 states that because we are sons, God has sent forth the Spirit of His Son into our hearts, crying out, "Abba Father!" But the passage goes on to say that we are like Isaac, children of promise! It is hard to find the "Isaacs" in the church today—there is an absence of joy in the body of Christ that is almost criminal. However, in Proverbs 17:22 the Bible says, "A merry heart does good, like medicine." And Ecclesiastes 3:4 tells us that there is a time to laugh!

God has made it possible for us to live with joy, where something wells up from the inside of us and bursts forth in a smiling countenance on our face. Your countenance, your face, testifies against you. It doesn't matter what you say! What you are really feeling shows on your face.

As much as we need the far-reaching power of an Abraham-sized faith, we also need the smile and laughter like that of Isaac. God has promised that He can turn mourning into dancing[4] and that He will release the oil of joy over the ashes of our broken lives.[5]

What kind of joy can you experience today?

The Laughter of Liberty

Isaac knew personally the laughter of liberty. So often we look at the story of Isaac and Abraham at Mount Moriah from the viewpoint of Abraham. However, we must remember that Isaac was standing there when Abraham looked at his servants and said, "I and the lad will go yonder to worship, and we will return." I believe the same faith that was in Abraham was also established in Isaac and that faith gave him the liberty to walk into anything with trust and joy.

It reminds me of the story of the pig and the little hen. The hen looked at the pig and said, "The farmer and his wife have been so good to us; why don't we offer them what we have for breakfast?" And the pig replied

indignantly, "For you it's just an offering; for me it's an ultimate sacrifice!"

As Isaac became aware of what God had required of him and of his father, something in Isaac kept him from running or fighting. The very same faith shown by his father enabled this strong young man to allow himself to be tied up and bound to an altar, facing an unreasonable death.

As heirs to the promise of Isaac, what was his in the natural is yours in the spiritual! The joy and the unbending faith of Isaac are yours! When Jesus came to earth, His first sermon proclaimed, "Blessed [happy] are the poor in spirit...the meek...the merciful...."[6] Everything that we deserved, everything that would cause the Father to frown at you and me, came and fell upon Jesus at the cross.

We know that Jesus cried, "...My God, My God, why have You forsaken me?"[7] In the past you've likely heard preachers proclaim that God turned his back on Jesus. However, God was in Christ reconciling the world unto Him. Jesus was never cut off; He was never less than God, not even while He was on the cross! When the Bible says that God is "of purer eyes than to behold evil [iniquity], and cannot look on wickedness..." we must realize the Hebrew translation of the word "look" means "to regard [look] with pleasure" or with a smile.[8]

What is the difference between your look at a child who is obeying you and a child who is disobeying you? There is a look of favor for one and a stern countenance for the other. I don't believe Scripture indicates that God did not look at Jesus when He was dying on the cross. Much earlier, the Father had said of Him, "This is My beloved Son, in whom I am well pleased."[9] But for one moment, the displeasure of God fell on Jesus, and the Father could not smile at His Son.

Jesus' lifeless body was laid in a new tomb,[10] but three days later He got up out of that grave so the Father would never have to do anything but smile at us, His forgiven children. You are forgiven, not because you are good, not even because you have confessed your sins. You are forgiven because God in His sovereignty allowed His Son to pay the price for your sins. Although our God can exhibit wrath against sin, because of Jesus I'm not appointed to wrath.[11] I know that God floods me with love through the blood of Jesus!

The release of joy! It is an unspeakable gift and full of glory! Jesus' blood was all-encompassing, and I am in covenant with Him. That liberating joy can be upon every one who has received Christ as Savior.

Smile of the Supernatural

Rejoice and know that we are living in a day when God is about to do something different! God is about

to do something supernatural, unusual, and powerful. God is about to break forth anew in His promise to Isaac.

Every part of Isaac's life was supernatural! His birth was supernatural; his rescue from Mount Moriah was supernatural. Even in the selection of Rebekah as his wife, a divine arrangement gave supernatural guidance.[12] And when he founded the city of Beersheba, God burst forth a brand-new well that still exists today.[13]

When you stand as an heir to the promise of Isaac, you have not only the laughter of liberty flowing out of you, but also the smile of the supernatural released in you, the very power of God. His promise stands for us: "For a mere moment I have forsaken you, but with great mercies I will gather you. With a little wrath I hid My face from you for a moment; but with everlasting kindness I will have mercy on you...."[14]

As parents and grandparents, we can sometimes be infuriated by our children. Nothing can make you angrier than your child! Maybe they have brought in all low grades. Maybe your son didn't mow the lawn, and your daughter didn't clean up her room. Sometimes you find yourself initially saying, "You're not getting another thing out of me."

I am so glad God doesn't treat us this way! When we bring our failures and "trash" of life to Him, the loving God of the universe says, "Wait just a minute;

don't worry! I may not like the negative things you do, but I love you and not only have I removed your transgressions (sins) from you 'as far as the east is from the west,'[15] but My mercy will be with you every day of your life."[16]

It is that same mercy that extends into your heart when you embrace that drug-addicted son or daughter. It is the same reason you have lovingly said to that wayward child, "Yes, you can come home." That's a measure of Abba's love.

The Hug of His Protection

Isaac reveled in God's abundant protection for him. Besides the obvious mercy God granted him at Mount Moriah, God also provided a bridge of peace between him and a potential enemy, Abimelech, and consistently provided water to supply Isaac's family and herds, even when traveling in dry and barren lands.

Isaiah 54:17 gives us such vital hope as we face our own difficulties: "'No weapon formed against you shall prosper, and every tongue which rises against you in judgment you shall condemn. This is the heritage of the servants of the Lord, and their righteousness is from Me,' says the Lord."

It has been said that there is no stronger need in childhood than the need for a father's protection. What

a blessing for us, knowing that we can't lose with the loving Father lingering nearby! Isaac learned he could trust his Father with anything in his life. Reach out in faith and take Abba's joyful gifts; feel His loving smile upon you as His child. The warmth of His love can break through any turmoil you may feel or experience.

Chapter 6

When Abba
Corrects—Jacob

Many years ago Dr. Charles Sullivan preached in my church. This dear friend is a brilliant man, a great preacher, and an executive in the Indiana Baptist Convention. A marvelous speaker, he has a voice that could knock out the back wall of any church sanctuary—without a microphone!

Along with his incredible voice, what you noticed about him almost immediately was the gentle tremble in his right hand. My first impression was that it was simply the result of his aging years. Sitting at breakfast with him one morning, I asked in my usual "shy" way, "Charles, tell me about that tremble in your hand."

"Well," he started, "I was called to preach at a young age, but I said 'no' to God. I was on my way to Baylor Medical School with a scholarship, and I was going to

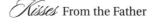

be a surgeon. I was going to be rich, and I was going to be a doctor!

"One Sunday night, God said, 'Charles, I'm calling you,'" and Dr. Sullivan described how a wrestling match of sorts ensued between them. My friend shook his head sadly and told me, "I walked out of that church and said to God, 'I'm not going to be a preacher!'

"I woke up the next morning, and my right hand was shaking. When I saw my trembling limb, I thought, *No one would want someone with a shaky hand to perform surgery on them*, and felt that to obey God was my best and only choice."

To heal a trembling hand is not a difficult task for the Lord. Nothing is impossible to Him. Yet, when we disobey God, we leave little room for Him to do anything for us. This is also true when it comes to healing. The Bible tells us, "to be carnally minded is death...."[1] Our disobedience to God only brings about the most difficult circumstances. However, our submission to Him reveals the depths of His love for us.

The Wrestling

It is a loving Father who is willing to engage us, letting us discover for ourselves what blessing awaits us in His perfect plan.

Our Father loves us, and so He will undoubtedly "spank" in the spirit, chasten, and correct His children.[2] Hebrews 12:8 confirms that "if you are without chastening...then you are illegitimate and not sons." The simple conclusion of this verse is that if you have walked through life without ever feeling the corrective hand of God or hearing His Spirit correct you, a serious heart examination is in order! You should see if you've ever yielded your life to Christ!

The good news is that if you have problems, difficulties, heartaches, heartbreaks, disappointments, or failures, you can focus your attention upon God, our loving Father, and He will perfect all of the things that concern you. But they will be perfected on His terms. He will correct you according to His Word. He will bring the conviction of the Holy Spirit that will wrestle with the carnality that holds you back from His best.

In this section of this book, we have been looking at the Old Testament fathers as examples of our heavenly Father's character. But we also see in these great patriarchs the characteristics that our precious Father wants to grow in us. Abraham demonstrated a towering faith that even looked into the future and to Calvary. Isaac's life showed an abounding joy, unspeakable and full of glory.

Moving on to Jacob, we see the power of God released, but not like we normally envision His greatness revealed. Jacob experienced the chastening hand of Abba.

> *Then Jacob was left alone; and a Man wrestled with him until the breaking of the day. Now when He saw that He did not prevail against him, He touched the socket of his hip [the hollow of his thigh]; and the socket of Jacob's hip was out of joint as He wrestled with him.*
>
> *And He [the Lord] said, "Let me go, for the day breaks." But he [Jacob] said, "I will not let you go unless you bless me!"*
>
> *So He said to him, "What is your name?" And he said, "Jacob."*
>
> *And He said, "Your name shall no longer be called Jacob, but Israel; for you have struggled with God and with men, and have prevailed."*
>
> *Then Jacob asked, saying, "Tell me Your name, I pray." And He said, "Why is it that you ask about My name?" And He blessed him there.*
>
> *And Jacob called the name of the place Peniel: "For I have seen God face to face, and my life is preserved."*
>
> *Just as he crossed over Penuel the sun rose on him, and he limped on his hip."*
>
> Genesis 32:24-31

The story is so simple, and yet so profound. Allow me to revert back to childhood as we examine Jacob's relationship with Abba Father. Do you remember the short words and simple phrases of your very first reading books and the famous adventures of Dick and Jane? Let's consider Jacob in the same straightforward way.

See Jacob Run

It has been said, "If in trouble, find your two feet and fly!" Nearly all his life, this patriarch took a version of this statement as his unspoken motto and ran from God. In Genesis 28, we do find him on a rare path of obedience, following his father's direction to find a wife of his own people. Jacob obediently began his journey, and one night he went to sleep with a rock as his pillow. A powerful experience followed, as God appeared to him. An angelic vision, a glimpse of glory, and a promise from God interrupted his sleep. When he awoke, he was filled with praise for God and a deep sense of awe. "Surely the Lord is in this place, and I did not know it," he said.

It seemed his life was on the right track, escaping the deception and restlessness of his youth. But a few years later, with wives and children in tow, he hit the road again and his running continued.

Sometimes running from God, sometimes running out of fear of his brother, Esau, or other times running from his destiny, finally one day he ran smack into God!

See Jacob Fight

I believe a transformation took place even as Jacob wrestled with God on that dark night. I believe the longer Jacob fought, the more he desired to have God's blessing and covering over his life.

Some people may say indignantly, "I'd surely never lift my hand to fight with my own Maker!" Perhaps you are already in a struggle right now. Maybe you are fighting the Word of God, the praise of God, the call of God, or the ministry of God upon your life. It is time to turn your fight into a battle for peace, grabbing the hem of His holy garment and crying, "O God, I'll do whatever you want—just bless me!"

The great poet and statesman James Weldon Johnson wrote a sermon reflecting upon the spiritual struggle faced by the Prodigal Son that could apply to Jacob's experience. Johnson proclaimed of the boy, "Young man—Young man—Your arm's too short to box with God."[3]

Jacob wrestled and fought against the God of the universe, and did it with all his might.

See Jacob Hurt

One of the popular fads that arose in the late twentieth century and has survived to this day is the professional wrestling craze. No doubt many a parent has picked up a TV remote on a Saturday afternoon, trying in vain to find something on the television other than grown men in shorts crazily throwing each other around a ring like circus performers! Their techniques are carefully honed so they appear to be doing enormous damage to their opponent, while actually there is minimal harm done. They talk the talk, but much of the fighting is staged. Fighting in the real world involves the goal of putting out your best punch and letting all your energy follow it!

But the Lord needed only to simply reach out and touch the hollow of Jacob's thigh. The minute He did, Jacob's leg went out of joint.

See Jacob Change

The next step for Jacob was to make a desperate lunge and cling to God.[4] The Lord looked at him and said, "Let me go, for the day breaks."[5] Jacob was fighting God only moments before, but now he is holding on to Him and begging, "I'm not letting go until You bless me! I'm staying for the blessing!"

Some believers never receive what they ask for from God because they give up asking too soon.[6] God sometimes breaks up our plans and interrupts our timetables and is on the verge of blessing us when we start whining and walk away. Maybe you were one mile from home when you stopped. Maybe you were just about to get your diploma from the school of hard knocks.

If that describes you, then it is time to realize that His hand *has* been upon you, not to hurt you, but to correct you; not to blast you, but to bless you. You may be in the throes of disaster right now—not just a canoe, but a Titanic-sized turmoil in your life. The good news is that a life raft of deliverance is already on its way, a threefold supply of grace.

A New Position

Who are you? What do people think when they see you coming? Do they exclaim, "There's a born-again, growing Christian," or do they think, *Watch out! Gossip, liar, thief, whiner—coming this way?*

In Genesis 32:27, God said to Jacob, "What is your name?" Of course, Jacob's name in Hebrew would have been "Ya'aqob," which literally means "heel-catcher"[7] or heel grabber. This name, given at his birth when he struggled to get ahead of his firstborn twin brother, followed him throughout his life, as later Jacob would steal the birthright and the blessing of Esau.[8]

But God looked at him, seeing the heel-grabbing, deceiving, lying trickster, and proclaimed, "You shall no longer be Ya'aqob. That is not your destiny, but you shall be Israel, prince of God." He literally spoke prophetically over Jacob, saying, "Your name has represented your character, but that's not who you really are. I've looked ahead, and you will be Israel."

It is time for us to confess who we are. As children of God, we can say, "I'm a joint heir with Jesus Christ! I belong to Him! I have a destiny beyond the skies. I'm somebody in Christ Jesus." We're so eager to continue to condemn ourselves as "no-good, lousy sinners." That's who we were *before* we met Christ. Once a person is saved, the Bible never calls the new believer a low-down, sorry sinner! You are a saint, 100 percent righteous, born anew, and a high priest of heaven.[9] God is your Father; you're the object of His affection! Quit confessing who you were, and start confessing who you are!

A New Power

Genesis 32:28 records God's further words to Jacob: "...you have struggled with God and with men, and have prevailed."

While the King of the universe easily had the power to win this wrestling contest, instead He said, "Guess what, Jacob—you won."

You can imagine Jacob's astonishment. "Won? How could this be?" he is probably wondering. But looking up into the face of his opponent, he suddenly understands. The victory has become his because his ability to run around manipulating things in his own power is gone. All he would know in the future would be the power and influence of His Father.

A New Perception

When Jacob got up from that wrestling circle with God, he was a new man. He had a new perception of God. He exclaimed later, "...I have seen God face to face, and my life is preserved."

He realized that God didn't want to kill him or to cripple him for life; He wanted to save him! Jacob discovered a truth we often miss: To fear God does not mean to be afraid of Him. To fear Him means to reverence Him. Perhaps you've found yourself quaking and cringing at the thought of your Father God looking at you with a scowl. Maybe you were a victim of abuse, and you've unconsciously looked at God as you did your abusive relative or father.

That's not Abba God! The only hurt He gives out is the hurt of correction—a hurt that heals! Just like open-heart surgery brings an element of pain to the body but renews the life of the patient, even so does God's corrective touch bring healing to you.

Jacob got up the next morning, and the Bible says he limped along. We will never really know how long Jacob limped on that leg, but we can clearly see that the corrective hand of God changed him for life. I often picture Jacob getting up morning after morning, saying, "Thank You, Lord! I was wounded, but now I'm worshipping. I was limping, but now I'm living. I may have been hurt, but now I'm whole. I may have been broken, but now I'm blessed."

The corrective hand of God comes to bring just that—correction. It is there to keep you on the path of His blessing. He corrects us so that our thinking can better align with His perfect will. Today, you may be hurting. Yet, there is a sunrise of blessing promised to you! An unknown poet said of Jacob,

> O gladly would I halting walk
> and marks of chastening bear
> if in the place of my defeat
> Thou wilst with Jacob bless me there.

Don't be afraid of your Father's correction. He is ready to whisper in your ear, "My grace is sufficient."[10]

Chapter 7

When Abba *Bridges* the Hurt—Joseph

A favored son with big dreams; a loving father who lavished gifts; jealous brothers filled with hate; the dreamer sold to slavery; the slave who became a prince over a nation. This is the Bible story of Joseph, a man who suffered much because he was willing to dream big, stand against evil, and accept the profound love of a doting father.

I believe that Joseph is more like Christ than anyone in the Old Testament. Arthur Pink, one of the great Old Testament scholars of our day, says there are 101 clear comparisons between the life of Joseph and the life of Jesus.[1] In studying Joseph's life, we can see clearly the Father's ultimate desire to bring good things out of the hurt that comes our way. Joseph even proclaimed that truth when he revealed himself to his brothers in Egypt, declaring, "Do not be grieved or angry with yourselves...it was God who sent me here...to save your lives!"[2]

A Grand Reunion

Genesis 45 picks up the story of Joseph right after he was reunited with his brothers after decades of trial, confusion, and promotion. His own brothers had sold him into slavery, and to ease their guilt, they no doubt assumed that Joseph had died long before. But now they had found their brother alive in Egypt, and his forgiveness toward them restored them fully! They brought the glad news to their father, Jacob.

> *Then they went up out of Egypt, and came to the land of Canaan to Jacob their father. And they told him, saying, "Joseph is still alive, and he is governor over all the land of Egypt." And Jacob's heart stood still, because he did not believe them.*
>
> *But when they told him all the words which Joseph had said to them, and when he saw the carts which Joseph had sent to carry him, the spirit of Jacob their father revived. Then Israel said, "It is enough. Joseph my son is still alive. I will go and see him before I die."*
>
> Genesis 45:25-28

This dear father Jacob had believed his son was dead all those years. At first, he didn't dare believe this shocking news. But Scripture shows that a turning point in his belief came when he heard Joseph's words relayed, and saw the wagons filled with wealth that Joseph had provided as gifts.

If you go back and read about those wagons in Genesis 45:21-23, you'll begin to understand how overwhelming it must have been to Jacob, who had suffered in famine for a long time. Joseph included 300 pieces of silver for Benjamin and garments for the entire family, along with twenty donkeys loaded with the good things of Egypt and grain, bread, and food for the journey.

Old Jacob had at first listened to the words of his sons, stunned and doubtful, but when he saw those wagons and donkeys loaded up and piled high, he knew this couldn't be a manufactured tale conjured up by deceitful sons. He knew somebody rich had come to his rescue. He knew somebody that had abundant resources and incredible devotion for him had come back into his life.

Accepting the Father's Provision

On a trip to Israel a few years ago, my wife, Paulette, and I had a different kind of a meal. We sat under a tent and ate a barbecue chicken dinner near an orange grove, which was presided over by a Bedouin. They reminded me of what the great patriarchs must have looked like. These nomads didn't look like they had much of anything in worldly wealth, but I found a 4-wheel-drive Land Rover hidden behind this particular tent!

After the meal, I was invited into the Bedouin's tent, and we exchanged bows and pleasantries. We talked about the Messiah and other topics he was interested in. But as we were ending our visit, he had an astonishing request. He humbly offered forty camels in trade for my wife, Paulette! (I later found out those animals were worth $40,000 each!)

When I quickly turned down his offer, he didn't seem distressed; he kissed me on both cheeks, and then said he'd accompany us back to the bus and send some fruit with us. I assumed we would be given a nice sack of oranges to carry along our way, but soon we found ourselves drowning in stalks of bananas, huge sacks of pomelos, and other exotic fruits. There must have been hundreds of pounds of fruit! We began distributing the fruit to everyone on our bus, but there was much left over! We finally took a side trip from our route and donated the remainder to an orphanage in Bethlehem.

The Father's Wagons

The generosity of my Bedouin friend is nothing compared to the goodwill of the One who sits on the heavenly throne, showering us with provision. Instead of looking at your problems, and instead of looking at all of the difficulties that you've had, it is time to realize that He has loaded up "wagons" of wealth for you and wants to spill His blessing all over you. The Father is more than able to bridge the hurt of the past and provide for your future. You'll find the Father's healing will be complete.

God's salvation and redemption are among the greatest of the Father's wagonloads of blessing. No matter what you've done, the blood of Jesus cleanses you from all sin.[3]

Yet another wagon He pulls into the life of the believer is one filled with the gifts and the fruit of the Holy Spirit.[4] As soon as we begin sampling of these incredible gifts, we look down a never-ending wagon train of blessing and remember the words of Paul, who said, "My God shall supply all your need according to His riches in glory by Christ Jesus."[5]

Finally Face to Face

You can imagine the scene when Jacob's eyes finally rested upon his long-lost son after years of loneliness and grief. Joseph met him in his chariot, and they fell upon each other weeping. You could see him grabbing his daddy's trembling hands, covering his face with kisses and saying, "Welcome home, Daddy! You'll never lack anything again; we'll take care of everything. All your wandering is over. You've slept your last night in a tent. You will have plenty of food. You're not going to

have to worry about marauders; nobody's going to steal from you anymore, Daddy. Everything's all right now."

This story reminds me that the heavenly Father's provision for me doesn't end here on earth. A great reunion awaits me in heaven! One day I'm going to walk up Hallelujah Boulevard, and the One who loved me and gave Himself for me is going to be there. I will see His nail-pierced hands open wide to embrace me, and He'll say, "Welcome home, Son! You will never be sick again; you'll never have a shortage in your life again; you'll never hurt again. Welcome home!"

Chapter 8

When Abba
Comes Singing

Isaiah could hardly see through the tears that poured from his eyes.[1] Uzziah, his beloved king and friend, had died suddenly. So fine a king he had been! I can imagine them growing close together through the years. Perhaps they had dreamed of Yahweh's kingdom coming on earth. Together, prophet and king dreamed of doing the work of Yahweh.

But now this vision, this dream, of Isaiah's was lying in a coffin. The throne of Judah was now empty, and hope died in his heart.

It is very likely that peace fled and the national conscience trembled in worry. The socially charged surrounding nations sometimes threatened the peace. The uneasiness must have hung like a storm cloud over the country. And in the middle of his personal grief, Isaiah began to recognize that people were looking to

him for an answer. After all, he was the prophet at court. He was the one who had access to the king. He was the one who was supposed to speak for God.

Week after week, Isaiah had thundered forth with the judgment of God. The words had been divinely given to him, and he knew that he was God's voice on the earth. But now in this time of pain, where was Yahweh? Isaiah wanted answers himself, but there were none given. Why the silence from heaven? Where was the word He had promised?

Isaiah, whose very name proclaimed "Yahweh saves,"[2] could not see salvation for Judah now that the king was dead. What would the prophet do?

Isaiah was in prayer just outside the temple when suddenly the doors opened, the veil hiding the Holy of Holies was withdrawn, and the Lord gave the discouraged prophet an insight into the invisible spiritual world. He granted him a transforming experience with the glory of God.[3]

In an instant the unspeakable swept over Isaiah, and he would do the boldest, most unthinkable act.

Yahweh was said to abide in the Holy of Holies in the magnificent Temple of Solomon. No one was allowed to go beyond the heavy veil hanging in front of the ark except the high priest, and then he was allowed there only once a year on the Day of Atonement. Isaiah had heard and even prophesied that no one could see the Lord and live.

At this juncture Isaiah decided to go into the Holy of Holies, partly because he was determined to ask God why so splendid a king had to die. And if Isaiah died in there, so be it!

I can picture Isaiah as he ascended the steps of the temple area. While its brilliance was always blinding, today it seemed especially so as its white and gold exterior blazed forth. From far away the golden crown of the temple looked like fire. He hurried quickly past the bronze altar where the blood of thousands of animals had been shed. He passed through the Holy Place and saw the shewbread illuminated by the fire of the seven-fold lampstand. And there, in front of him, hung the magnificent, now-withdrawn veil, and life or death was on the other side. Isaiah made his way inside.

Instantly, he fell to his knees. He lifted his tear-swollen eyes to see a glowing light above the blood-encrusted mercy seat. The light rose and hovered over Isaiah like a cloud. The glory, or *kabowd*,[4] washed over him, and the weight of God's majesty kept him from moving.

Isaiah actually described the experience he had in this way:

> *In the year that King Uzziah died, I saw the Lord sitting on a throne, high and lifted up, and the train of His robe filled the temple. Above it stood seraphim;*

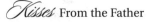

each one had six wings: with two he covered his face, with two he covered his feet, and with two he flew.

And one cried to another and said: "Holy, holy, holy is the Lord of hosts; the whole earth is full of His glory!" And the posts of the door were shaken by the voice of him who cried out, and the house was filled with smoke.

So I said: "Woe is me, for I am undone! Because I am a man of unclean lips, and I dwell in the midst of a people of unclean lips; for my eyes have seen the King, the Lord of hosts."

Isaiah 6:1-5

Isaiah had rushed to this place, leaving behind the palace with its empty throne. Now before him, he saw heaven's throne, full and alive with glory. He would testify that he "...saw the Lord, high and lifted up...."

Isaiah was about to receive the ultimate revelation of Yahweh! In those moments, he discovered that Yahweh did not want him to die from this experience, but wanted simply to use him. God revealed to Isaiah amazing things about Himself, the future, and the promise of a Messiah:

—He would be born of a virgin.[5]

—He would be a new kind of King with a new kingdom.[6]

—He would die as the sinners' substitute.[7]

—He would be the Wonderful Counselor, Mighty God, Everlasting Father, and Prince of Peace.[8]

Yahweh declared in clear tones, "I am coming to My people!" He was coming to redeem man, to reveal God as the light, to reign as King. Clearly, God's relationship to His people would be as an "everlasting Father." God was more than a sovereign reigning in majesty far above us all. He would come to His people and reveal Himself as the Father.

Isaiah awoke from his ecstasy with a sense of his sin. A blazing angel brought a hot coal to touch his mouth, and in a burst of cleansing and freedom, Isaiah felt the Father's forgiveness of his failures.

God then summoned Isaiah to service by crying, "Who will go for Us?" Only hours before, Isaiah wanted to quit, but his response to the Father was now, "Here am I! Send me." Isaiah did not view God as a tyrant who takes the lives of those He loves, but he entertained only a desire to serve this Father who sacrifices Himself for His children. The Father's heart cry was recorded for generations to read:

> But now, thus says the Lord, who created you, O Jacob, and He who formed you, O Israel: "Fear not, for I have redeemed you; I have called you by your name; you are Mine. When you pass through the waters, I will be with you; and through the rivers, they shall not overflow you. When you walk through the fire, you

shall not be burned, nor shall the flame scorch you. For I am the Lord your God, the Holy One of Israel, your Savior; I gave Egypt for your ransom, Ethiopia and Seba in your place. Since you were precious in My sight, you have been honored, and I have loved you; therefore I will give men for you, and people for your life. Fear not, for I am with you; I will bring your descendants from the east, and gather you from the west; I will say to the north, 'Give them up!' And to the south, 'Do not keep them back!' Bring My sons from afar, and My daughters from the ends of the earth— Everyone who is called by My name, whom I have created for My glory; I have formed him, yes, I have made him."

Isaiah 43:1-7

They Heard the Father's Song

After his powerful experience, Isaiah carefully recorded and prophesied the extent of God's tender love to His sons and daughters. But perhaps one of the most beautiful pictures of the care of God the Father is in the following promise.

Listen to Me, O house of Jacob, and all the remnant of the house of Israel, who have been upheld by Me from birth, who have been carried from the womb: Even to your old age, I am He, and even to gray hairs I will carry you! I have made, and I will bear; even I will carry, and will deliver you.

Isaiah 46:3,4

Isaiah's amazing experience and revelation of God as the Father dynamically changed his life. But he wasn't the only prophet who received this revelation. Throughout the major and minor prophets, we sense the heartache of a God who longed to spiritually father His children.

Jeremiah

The sensitive heart of this prophet realized that the same God who had sent a sinning Judah into captivity was coming with a new covenant for His children. Jeremiah saw God looking upon His people as "dear" and "pleasant," with a paternal pledge to always remember them. He speaks of a yearning heart of love for His child.

> *Is Ephraim My dear son? Is he a pleasant child? For though I spoke against him, I earnestly remember him still; therefore My heart yearns for him; I will surely have mercy on him, says the Lord.*
>
> Jeremiah 31:20

Hosea

One of the most poignant passages is found in Hosea, where his description of God as Father reveals the love, instruction, call, and healing offered by Him.

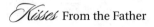

"When Israel was a child, I loved him, and out of Egypt I called My son. As they called them, so they went from them; they sacrificed to the Baals, and burned incense to carved images.

"I taught Ephraim to walk, taking them by their arms; but they did not know that I healed them. I drew them with gentle cords, with bands of love, and I was to them as those who take the yoke from their neck. I stooped and fed them.

"He shall not return to the land of Egypt; but the Assyrian shall be his king, because they refused to repent. And the sword shall slash in his cities, devour his districts, and consume them, because of their own counsels. My people are bent on backsliding from Me. Though they call to the Most High, none at all exalt Him.

"How can I give you up, Ephraim? How can I hand you over, Israel? How can I make you like Admah? How can I set you like Zeboiim? My heart churns within Me; my sympathy is stirred. I will not execute the fierceness of My anger; I will not again destroy Ephraim. For I am God, and not man, the Holy One in your midst; and I will not come with terror."

Hosea 11:1-9

Hosea's words are a great comfort to us. As you begin to walk in a closer relationship with your Abba Father, you will confidently learn to declare the following truths:

—I am loved; therefore, I am significant!

—I am called; therefore, I have purpose!

—I am taught; therefore, I can change!

—I am healed; therefore, I am whole!

Zephaniah

Some of the most tender words about Father God are found in Zephaniah. Yahweh pursued His wayward child, Israel, and diligently planned their restoration from captivity. He promised healing every step of the way. And the centerpiece for His plan is found in Zephaniah 3:17, for the lullaby of Abba is first promised in what some have called the John 3:16 of the Old Testament:

> *The Lord your God in your midst, the Mighty One, will save; he will rejoice over you with gladness, he will quiet you with His love, he will rejoice over you with singing.*

Several Scriptures talk of the Lord singing. For example, Hebrews 2:12 says, "...in the midst of the assembly I [Jesus] will sing praise to You." Other Scriptures, such as Ephesians 5:18-19, reveal that the believer has songs in one's heart that are inspired by the Holy Spirit. Often the result of singing praises to God is a powerful sense of His Presence in our midst.

Indeed, in my church we have experienced this on many occasions, as God's Spirit moved upon a soloist or group and spoke words of healing and comfort to the congregation. And although the entire congregation was ministered to, the power of God reached to individual hearts as though He were only speaking one on one to each of His children.

As leaders of worship at the Toronto Airport Christian Fellowship in Ontario, Canada, Jeremy and Connie Sinnott have also learned to listen to the Father's song and minister to others through it. They wrote of such an experience:

> One night at a renewal meeting in Toronto, we stepped off the platform and began to sing over the people lying on the floor.[9] We do this often, but this particular night one lady told us that just before we came to sing over her she had said to God, "I really need to know if You truly love me. Would it be possible for You to send someone to sing Your message of love over me?" No wonder she burst into tears when one of us walked over to her just then and knelt beside her to sing about His arms of love.
>
> Another woman experienced healing in the same way. She had been adopted as a child and had always had a deep sense of loneliness and abandonment. When the song "I Will Not Forget You" was sung over her, God assured her that "though a mother forgets the baby at her breast, I won't forget you."[10]

As our worship team sings over people receiving prayer, we often witness tears of release as God pours His love into them.... The sense of abandonment is gone, replaced by the assurance of their heavenly Father's unconditional love for them. When the fear of abandonment goes, the human spirit just automatically sings. Like the Scripture says, "Through each day the Lord pours His unfailing love upon me, and through each night I sing His songs, praying to God who gives me life" (Psalm 42:8 NLT).[11]

In Zephaniah 3:17 Zephaniah's use of the word "gladness," or "joy" (as the *King James Version* says), actually meant leaping or spinning wildly.[12] This concept of a Father God who is so enamoured with us that He not only sits quietly contemplating His love for us one moment, but in the next breaks into joyous dancing over us, is hard for us to comprehend. It surely smashes through any stained-glass traditional picture that we have in our minds concerning God!

Malachi

The Old Testament closes with the unique promises of Malachi. As quoted earlier, Abba's clear declaration and call to repentance is in Malachi 2:10:

> *Have we not all one Father? Has not one God created us? Why do we deal treacherously with one another by profaning the covenant of the fathers?*

Because God is uniquely our Father, our conduct toward each other should be upright. The covenant of Yahweh governs our relationships with our family of faith.

Again in Malachi 1:6, Yahweh speaks: "A son honors his father, and a servant his master. If then I am the Father, where is My honor? And if I am a Master, where is My reverence? says the Lord of hosts...." God indicates that He is dishonored by the way we treat Him and others. Malachi spends much time in his writings chastising the people for bringing second-rate offerings, for dealing with each other dishonorably, and for making light of the marriage covenant.

Jesus longed to make us understand the importance of our unity with each other as He prayed the Lord's Prayer, which begins, "Our Father...."[13] Notice, it begins in the plural, not the singular "*My* Father." To call Him Father is to embrace the whole family of God. Yahweh God observes our treatment of our brothers and sisters and takes it very seriously.

Malachi again reveals the tender yearnings of the heart of God in chapter 3.

> "*Bring all the tithes into the storehouse, that there may be food in My house, and try Me now in this," says the Lord of hosts, "If I will not open for you the windows of heaven and pour out for you such blessing that there will not be room enough to receive it.*

"And I will rebuke the devourer for your sakes, so that he will not destroy the fruit of your ground, nor shall the vine fail to bear fruit for you in the field," says the Lord of hosts; "and all nations will call you blessed, for you will be a delightful land," says the Lord of hosts.

"Your words have been harsh against Me," says the Lord, "Yet you say, 'What have we spoken against You?' You have said, 'It is useless to serve God; what profit is it that we have kept His ordinance, and that we have walked as mourners before the Lord of hosts? So now we call the proud blessed, for those who do wicked-ness are raised up; they even tempt God and go free.'"

Then those who feared the Lord spoke to one another, and the Lord listened and heard them; so a book of remembrance was written before Him for those who fear the Lord and who meditate on His name.

"They shall be Mine," says the Lord of hosts, "On the day that I make them My jewels. And I will spare them as a man spares his own son who serves him."

Malachi 3:10-17

The next word of the Father would come in person, in the arrival of His Son Jesus Christ upon the earth, who would be given the task of showing us the Father! But the purposeful love song of the Father never ends, as He joyfully gathers His children under His wing and showers us with a lullaby of grace and peace.

Do you hear His calming voice in your heart? In the words of author Steve Beard, may we all come to

experience more clearly the joys of being lovingly held "...in the hands of a singing God."[14]

SECTION THREE

Meet the *Father*

———⊷⊶———

Chapter 9

Abba Story:
Daughter of Abba

There was no end to her constant shame and embarrassment.[1] I can picture the scene twelve years earlier of this beautiful young woman being the prettiest girl in her circle of friends. She had only wanted to have a good time. The young Roman soldier was so handsome, and his stories of faraway exploits held her spellbound. She knew better, and yet, soon she was swept away in a love affair that could never be.

Eventually her lover was posted to another assignment, and she was left alone. At first, she feared she might be pregnant, but soon her womanly cycle began, to her relief. A week later, she was still hemorrhaging. It wasn't much, but it never stopped. She was infected with some disease. Yahweh was surely punishing her for her wayward behavior.

In her condition she was not welcome at synagogue or any of the great festivals in Jerusalem. No man

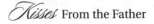

would have her in marriage, for she was considered cursed. Here she was, a daughter of Zion, unable to marry, and worst of all, unable to bear children! She would never know the joy of nursing her own child. She would never experience the loving embrace of a husband. She was all alone!

Every year, she sent inquiries to any new physician, seeking the latest in medical care. She endured much pain, but no one would treat her. She grew worse with every disappointment. Worst of all, Yahweh seemed far away. She could no longer attend the reading and teaching of Scripture. She could not participate in the beautiful worship of her religion. Even her own earthly father and mother could have nothing to do with her.

Oh, she thought often of taking her own life, but she feared that would only cause her to be cast into hell. She wept often in the night. She had no family, no friends, and no future. Life was an island of bitter solitude. Twelve lonely years had passed, and she was slowly dying. She did not know what to do.

Rumors began circulating about a young healing evangelist from Galilee named Yeshua. This man had opened blind eyes, unstopped deaf ears, made the crippled to walk, straightened twisted limbs, and healed all manner of illness. Some even dared to believe that this Jesus was the long awaited Messiah!

She heard the rumors as they circulated among the cadre of outcasts who were her companions in misery.

She did believe the Torah and the prophets. Messiah was a promise every child of Israel heard of and believed in from youth. She recalled the stories of Job and how Satan had afflicted him with a terrible disease, yet Job held onto God and in the end was restored and healed. She began to voice her hope to those other outcasts around her. Soon, she was silenced by their ridicule. How dare she think that someone like her could go approach someone like Yeshua! The law forbade her from going around other people lest she defile them. Who did she think she was anyway?

If she could only think of a verse of Scripture that would give her permission to go to this Yeshua! She could not legally go. They might even stone her to death for violation of the ceremonial law. Something inside her believed anyway! She was bleeding to death, so what did she have to lose? Let them scorn her and even let them kill her, but she had to try.

Veiling her face to protect herself from the stares of the crowd, she made her way to where Yeshua was supposed to pass by. She heard the cry, "Yeshua is coming!" She caught a glimpse of Him and, to her dismay, there beside Him was her pastor, the ruler of their synagogue! Oh, how she blushed with shame to think of exposing herself to this crowd!

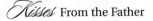

As she thought on these things, the crowd swept past her, pushing Yeshua along with them. He was almost out of sight now! What would she do? She mustered up her courage and ran toward the crowd. She pushed people aside and ignored their insults as they recognized "that cursed woman." She began to weep, and her veil flew off her head. She was always only inches from Him but could not get nearer. On her last attempt, she sprawled into the dust, and just in front of her face, the tassel of His prayer shawl dragged the ground. In one desperate moment, she pushed forward and seized the hem of His garment.

She suddenly felt as if a wind rushed over her body. Energy surged into her weak frame. In that one moment, she knew her bleeding had stopped! She had her miracle! She wept with joy and gratitude.

"Who touched Me?"

She heard His question, as did the throng around Him. Somehow, His power had been imparted to her, and she knew according to the law she was not to touch this Rabbi. Somehow He sensed a sick sinner had touched Him. He was calling for her, and she knew it. Would He rebuke her? Would He shame her? Would He smite her with a worse disease?

She lay shaking on the ground, fearful to look up. What a mess she was. Her face was streaked with tears and the dust of the street. Her clothes were disheveled and dirty. Her fear caused her to tremble violently now. Taking a breath, she finally looked up and found herself gazing directly into the tender eyes of Yeshua.

Love flooded her, washing over her lonely soul like a cool artesian spring. No one had looked upon her with kindness in a dozen years! She crawled into His shadow, confessing all of her failure and heartache in a wild rush of words and tears. As she did, she found a lifetime of grief and loneliness had disappeared, and she poured out her thanks.

Lying still now, she felt a touch on her shoulder, and His strong hands pulled her to her feet. She looked again into His eyes. The look reminded her of long-ago days when she would gaze into her abba's face as a little girl. Her daddy had always made her feel special. In this moment before Yeshua, she forgot her age, for in her heart she was like a little child encountering the love of a father.

Yeshua spoke. "Daughter," He said. She was again the pure little girl who had gladdened the heart of her father before sin had taken its toll. "Daughter," He said. She was now part of a forever family. "Daughter," He said. She had an Abba, a Daddy as her Lord. Trust, healing, and peace filled her life. She knew she belonged, and she never would be the same again.

My friend, whatever you may have done or been through, Jesus has come to take you to your Abba! He

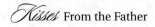

loves you and will forgive your failures. He has come to make you family. The scars of your past can be healed, and you can live at peace with Him. You simply need to get up from where you are, press through the crowded streets of your life, and touch Him! Your days of isolation, guilt, and failure will be over. He has come to show you your heavenly Father.

Chapter 10

The Father's *Face*

Dr. Manuel Scott, one of the foremost African-American preachers in America in the twentieth century, had the privilege of helping his daughter rear his grandson. I heard him tell of the day that his grandson announced that he wanted a pair of the most popular brand-name tennis shoes, at a price of over $135.

When Dr. Scott bought them for the boy, his daughter was livid. "Daddy," she ranted, "how am I ever going to train this boy if you buy him everything he wants, if you indulge his every wish? He just asks, and you melt and give him everything he wants."

Smiling, he said calmly, "Now, honey, don't get excited," but the daughter interrupted once again.

"But, Daddy, how am I ever going to teach him any responsibility?"

He said, "Honey, I didn't buy him those shoes because he deserved them. I bought them for him for all those times he came into my office, crawled up in my lap, and said, 'I love you, Papaw.'"

It is time for each of us to realize that Christianity is not a responsibility, but a *response* to the love of God the Father. Perhaps you are a refugee from lifeless legalism. Perhaps you have walked out of the frigid freezer of fundamentalism where you have heard about God's grace, but as soon as you got some, you ended up under the law. However, there is freedom and abundance in the Father's house!

The God you serve has done amazing things for you, not because you earned it, deserved it, could keep the rules, or showed you could act responsibly. Your heavenly Father above has eyes full of mercy and love.

As we have seen, God chose to use illustrations, object lessons, and examples with the Old Testament saints to demonstrate His Fatherhood. But when Jesus arrived on earth, He brought a powerful and clear revelation of the Father.

As Phillip said, "...Lord, show us the Father..."[1] and Jesus was more than ready to comply!

"...He who has seen me," said Jesus to Phillip, "has seen the Father...."[2]

We didn't walk on the earth with the disciples, so you and I haven't seen Jesus with the eye of the flesh, but we can say with Job, "...I know that my Redeemer lives...Whom I shall see for myself, and my eyes shall behold...."[3]

When I retrace Jesus' life on earth, I must start at the manger. Looking into the cradle, I see the face of One whom the Bible calls "everlasting Father."[4] When I see Him as an adult, His face turned with compassion upon the poor, I see Him as a Provider, taking bread and feeding the hungry. I see Him setting the captive free. The only time I ever really observe His anger in the Gospels is when He sees the religious crowd trying to bring people under the bondage of their rules and laws.

I see Him touching blind eyes, unstopping deaf ears, and setting demon-captive people free. I see Him looking at fallen women and raising them up and saying, "...go and sin no more."[5] I see Him walking about doing good. Even when the religious crowd finally can't stand it anymore, and they arrest Him, rip His back with a whip, and nail Him to a cross, I know that in that bloody face shines the love of my Father for me.

You may say, "Where was the Father when Jesus hung on the cross?" Don't you think for one minute that our Father was beating His own Son. He was in His Son, receiving as the Father the punishment we deserve. What I mean is this: As Paul later explained in Colossians 2:9 KJV, "God was in Christ, reconciling the world unto Himself." The *New Living Translation* says it this way: "For in Christ the fullness of God lives in a human body...." If that is true, which it is, then it could be said that the whole Trinity was crucified. I can look

at the bloody face of Jesus of Nazareth, His head crowned with thorns, tears streaming down His cheeks, and say, "My Father" because Jesus said, "...He who has seen Me has seen the Father...."[6]

The Father's grace is so wonderful! His provision is so magnificent that people who curse Him, people who refuse to believe in Him, can breathe His air, drink His water, live on His planet, and He still appeals to them with a nail-pierced hand, "Come to Me!" The church should be a hospital for sinners, a place for scalawags, a place for failures to have a new beginning, a place for sin to be washed away by the blood of Jesus Christ.

Perhaps you have been trying to perform for somebody all your life. Maybe you've tried to do a list of rules. Know that your heavenly Father just wants you to come and enjoy His Presence and love on Him a little bit, dance before Him a little bit, and sing to Him. He just wants to take pleasure in who you are.

My two girls and my son will likely read this book, and so they will learn a little secret: They could have received more favors from their mother and me! All they needed to do was ask! If you are a parent reading this, no doubt you agree; so many times you long to help your children, but you have to wait because you know that somehow they have to work through some stuff on their own.

What if your child needed a kidney and you had one that matched? Most parents wouldn't give it a second thought; you'd say to the surgeon, "Start cutting!" Jesus knew this sacrificial love was inherent in loving parents, and that's why He said, "If you then, being evil, know how to give good gifts to your children, how much more will your Father who is in heaven give good things to those who ask Him!"[7]

In Jesus Christ, I see tangible evidence of who the Father is. I need a Father who can see the greatness in me and not just my weaknesses. And John 14:12 shows that He does believe in us! "Most assuredly, I say to you, he who believes in Me, the works that I do he will do also; and greater works than these he will do, because I go to My Father."

I know friends who have struggled after elusive perfection all their lives. Maybe all they heard was, "You made a B; you should have gotten an A. You scored a touchdown; you ought to have made the extra point. You ran to third base; you should have made it to home plate!"

I know a Father who can look at anyone like this and say, "You thought my Son Jesus did some great works; you are going to do greater works because I am going to My Father, and He's going to pour His Spirit out on you." He sees the potential in us all.

I also need a Father who will talk to me. In John 14:14 He promises, "If you ask anything in My name, I will do it." My Father not only hears my cry and answers my call, but also responds, speaking to me in my spirit and by His powerful Word.

The Father's Face Is Near

My Father will never leave me alone. John 14:18 gives yet another promise: "I will not leave you orphans; I will come to you." In the loneliest, darkest, saddest, and even suicidal moments of my own life, He has never failed to come.

At times, I hear Him in a still, small voice behind me saying, "This is the way; walk in it." Sometimes He appears "with skin on" through the care and concern of a friend, but His voice clearly speaks through that tenderness. Very often He assures me of His Presence through great music that touches and stirs the soul. On other occasions, it is a Christian radio or television broadcast or sometimes even a secular movie through which God pops a window open in my soul and speaks. He promises, "I will not leave you orphans."

My buddy Rick White and I have been friends for thirty years. One time Rick was preaching at his church using that oft-told story about the young boy who stood on the beach, anxiously picking up starfish one

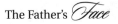

by one that were washed up on the shore and throwing them back into the safety of the surf. A cynical old man walked up to the young boy and, seeing the thousands of stranded starfish upon the beach, said, "Son, do you really believe that what you are doing is making any difference at all?" The little boy, grasping one more of the helpless creatures, said, "It makes a difference to this one."

Rick told the story, and it had a profound effect on his congregation that day. But the story especially hit home with Rick's teenage daughter, Torie. She is a different kind of a young person. There is something in her already that is calling her to missions. She left shortly after for a trip to Romania, where their group ministered in an orphanage. There she met four little orphan girls. These four little ones had only one pair of shoes that they would trade off wearing on different days of the week. Among the children, one stood out to Torie—a little girl named Alona.

Torie came home to the States, and the night she returned, she sat on her parents' bed and announced, "Mom and Dad, I think we need to adopt Alona."

Rick immediately jumped to calm this radical idea: "Torie, we aren't talking about a puppy here. You are talking about a human being." Rick began to explain how the world was filled with thousands of orphans

and that it wasn't possible to set up the perfect environment for each one.

But Torie looked him in the eye and said, "But, Daddy, what about the starfish?"

God spoke to Rick and Patti in their hearts, and they made their way to Romania. Just a few months later, they took eight-year-old Alona into their home, and Torie had a new little sister, rescued by love and persistence.

I thought about our Father looking at us down here, impoverished in reality and homeless in eternity, not able to save ourselves, as helpless as we could be, not one thing we could do. We were all orphans. The Father said, "I must go to rescue them."

Jesus said, "Lord, I want to go."

I imagine the Father saying, "They won't all come."

Jesus could have replied, "What if one comes?"

Then the Father agreed, "Go to the cross and save My children!"

I am overwhelmed to have a heavenly Father like that.

The internationally famous author Ernest Hemingway wrote a story about a man and his boy named Paco.[8] This father and son became distanced from each other emotionally. In anger, the father finally ran the boy out of the house. After a few months, the father softened up, knew he had done wrong, and decided that he would try to get his boy back. The father launched a long and arduous search to find his beloved son. After many months the father's efforts to locate Paco continued to be fruitless.

As a last resort, the grieving father placed a notice in the personal columns of *El Liberal,* a Madrid newspaper, hoping that Paco would see the ad and respond. The ad read, "Dear Paco, Please meet me in front of the newspaper office at noon. All is forgiven. Love, Father."

As Hemingway tells the story, the next day at noon, a squadron of Guardia Civil had to be sent to the front of the newspaper office to disperse the 800 "Pacos" who showed up seeking forgiveness from their fathers!

Our heavenly Father's face is turned toward us. Come to Him with all your past and your sins—He is the only One who can forgive, cleanse, and adopt you into His family. I'm glad that I don't have to do one thing to make Him love me.

Chapter 11

Gifts From the Father's Hand

When Howard Hughes died, he left behind a fortune estimated to be worth over $2 billion. What he failed to leave behind was a valid last will and testament. So the U.S. Treasury Department and the Supreme Court had the daunting task of dividing the estate among twenty-two legitimate heirs and several corporations, a process that took seven years.[1]

I have heard that among other famous people who have died without a valid will are Presidents Abraham Lincoln (who was a lawyer and should have known better!), Andrew Johnson, and Ulysses S. Grant, as well as famed painter Pablo Picasso.

Though most people are aware that they need a will in order to leave their worldly goods as a gift to their families, many Americans don't have one (as high as 74 percent according to one recent survey).[2]

God's Last and Ongoing Will

When Jesus was leaving this earth to return to heaven, He made sure to bestow His precious inheritance upon us. His Word is His will, but one particular Scripture that I think of as His "last will and testament" of sorts is found in John 14:16-18.

> *"And I will pray the Father, and He will give you another Helper [Comforter], that He may abide with you forever—the Spirit of truth, whom the world cannot receive, because it neither sees Him nor knows Him; but you know Him, for He dwells with you and will be in you. I will not leave you orphans; I will come to you."*
>
> *Jesus spoke those words because the time had come for Him to go away. A little later on He told them, "...It is expedient [better] that I go away: for if I go not away, the Comforter will not come unto you; but if I depart, I will send him unto you."*[3]

As we have discovered, the first work of the Holy Spirit in your life is to show you your relationship with the Father. When you get saved, He sends forth His Spirit into your heart. The first thing the Holy Ghost says to you is "Abba, Father." In receiving that word from Him, you are able to break the spirit of bondage off your life and embrace a heavenly Father. You tear fear out of your heart, and all of a sudden what the Spirit of God cried in your heart (according to Galatians 4:6) you are now able to cry out in freedom, "Abba, Father! Abba, Father!"

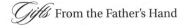

However, the Comforter's role continues, bringing to us all that is our promised inheritance of heaven. In a closer look at John chapters 14-16, we discover the incredible works of the Holy Spirit that you and I need desperately.

Comfort

We need the comfort of the Father. The very word "Comforter" comes from two Greek words *para* and *kaleo*,[4] or *parakletos* in the Greek language. Such an interesting and multilayered word it is! It means one who is summoned alongside. It is the word used for a coach. It is the word used for a legal lawyer, an advocate who pleads your case. It is the word used for an encourager. It is the word used for a teacher.[5] In 1 John 2:1 it is translated *advocate:* "...if anyone sins, we have an Advocate with the Father, Jesus Christ the righteous."

The word also could be defined "cheerleader." It brings to my mind the picture of a football stadium full of cheering fans when a team is winning (or if they are good fans, when it is losing!).

In ancient Greece when the foot races were about to end, those who had coached the athletes would make their way to the side of the track. As sprinters, fatigued from the race, would be coming toward the final home stretch, those who had coached them would run alongside and cheer them on. "Run! Run! Run!" they might say. "You can win! You can finish! You can make it!"

A modern day example of that was one of the most striking moments of the 1992 Olympics. In the men's 400-meter run, Great Britain's Derek Redmond was coming to the end of his race when he suddenly lurched and broke his stride—he had severely pulled a hamstring muscle. The crowd gasped, watching in agony as he struggled to his feet in an obvious determination to finish. He fell again, then stood again, vainly attempting to limp toward the finish line.

Suddenly, a big burly man, not conditioned like a sprinter, bounded over the wall out of the stands. Coming alongside the injured runner, the man put his arms around Derek and half-ran, half-walked, hobbled, and carried him across the line. The big man was Derek's own father.

When you were lost and injured (emotionally and spiritually) and couldn't get home, your Father came out of heaven in the person of Jesus Christ and was abused, hanged on the cross for you, and died for you; then He was raised from the dead for you. He went to heaven and sent the Holy Spirit back here to help you up.

In your Christian life, you will have falls. While in this world, you still live in a body that is subject to temptation and failure. Many times you've probably spiritually pulled your hamstring and gone down, thinking, *I can't get up from here. I don't want to get up from here. It hurts too bad. The race is too long.* Then you have felt an everlasting arm reach under you and

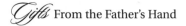

lift you up and take you in.[6] That is the beauty of the comfort, companionship, and encouragement of Abba.

Communication

Human relationships are not always perfect. You can't always count on them, but I have a heavenly Father who doesn't slumber, doesn't sleep,[7] will never go away, will never do anything wrong, will never fail me, will never let me down. The Bible tells me that my Comforter will hear what the Father is saying, and He will speak those things to me.

We all need a Father who will communicate. The Word says in John 14:25, "But the Helper, the Comforter, the Holy Spirit, whom the Father will send in My name, He will teach you all things, and bring to your remembrance all things that I said to you." If you go on over to John 16:13, it says, "However, when He, the Spirit of truth, has come, He will guide you into all truth; for He will not speak on His own authority, but whatever He hears He will speak; and He will tell you things to come." I have a Father who will talk to me.

What does a father say to his children? What do you want your heavenly Father to say? Do you need to hear, "I love you"? God surely does love you, for John wrote, "For God so loved the world that He gave...."[8] The Father exclaims over you, "I love you."

Do you long to hear, "I'm going to take care of you; I'm going to be here for you"? He promised this to you also, saying, "...I will never leave you nor forsake you."[9]

God speaks to you out of the Bible, the Book of books. He can also speak to your spirit through His Holy Spirit. Isaiah 30:21 says, "Your ears shall hear a word behind you, saying, 'This is the way, walk in it,'...." If you will listen, God is speaking.

If you are in a valley, know that He is speaking to you, saying, "...fear no evil...."[10] He can speak to you on that mountaintop. He can speak to you in your circumstances. You've got a Father who will tell you clearly, "Listen well."

Conviction

As we read on in John 16:8 AMP, God's coming would convict (and convince) the world of sin, of (His) righteousness, and of (the coming) judgment. As unusual as it sounds, part of the Father's gift to us is His convicting and disciplining of our lives!

He doesn't come to convict you of sin in order to beat you down. He sent the Holy Spirit to make you righteous. He came to live in your spirit that was spiritually dead because of sin, and He raised it from the dead to new life in Him.[11] As His child, you've got His righteousness and His power in your life.[12] The Father's righteousness is your breastplate and your protector.[13]

He convicts us of sin so He can say, "I pardon you!" He convicts us of righteousness so He can proclaim, "I've come to promote you, to make you something." And He convicts us of judgment to promise, "I've come to protect you."

Calling

"What is my purpose in life?" "Why am I on this planet?"

These questions aren't isolated to just high school graduates or young college students. We all are in search of meaning and purpose in our lives. And God brings that to us—a spirit of adventure and challenge to take up His cross and follow His will!

Remember, John 16:13 says, "However, when He, the Spirit of truth, has come, He will guide you into all truth; for He will not speak on His own authority, but whatever He hears He will speak; and He will tell you things to come. Verse 14 continues, "He will glorify Me, for He will take what is Mine and declare it to you." We need a Father who challenges us to go on.

Jesus promised He would "guide" us, which brings to mind how He guided the children of Israel in a pillar of cloud by day and fire by night through the treacherous wilderness on their journey to the Promised Land.[14] Face it—pursuing God's truth is an amazing journey! However, too many believers grab on to the first truth they learn

about and then sit on it, like a stubborn donkey in the middle of a trail. It is this attitude that keeps churches and believers from achieving unity. Rather than seeking after signs or clinging to a single doctrine, believers must journey on with Jesus and seek His heart.

Following the Father's Voice

Jesus' challenge to us, His calling, is to "Follow on." What an exciting call! Jesus acknowledges us as joint heirs with Him, saying literally, "What is Mine is yours."[15] And the Holy Spirit wants to guide you into the treasure chest of what God has for you.

We have for too long kept our hands behind our backs, afraid to plunge them into the fruit basket of the Spirit, not opening up the presents God has for us. There is so much to experience, so much to see. Jesus cries, "Follow on."

A simple, yet potentially double-edged Ashanti proverb begins Javaka Steptoe's picture book entitled "In Daddy's Arms, I Am Tall," a powerful collection of poems celebrating African-American fathers. The proverb reads, "When you follow in the path of your father, you learn to walk like him."[16]

In Jesus' arms I don't have to worry about the future! The future is in the hands of my Father. He will whisper in my ear, and He will say, "This is what I'm going to do if you will trust Me and step out in faith. My gifts are here to help you live in peace and joy."

Chapter 12

Sitting at Abba's Knee

"Special speaker tonight! Hear Jesus of Nazareth at the Mount of Olives!"

While you could imagine signs such as this advertising Jesus' great Sermon on the Mount, the truth is that the word of His powerful message and straightforward delivery had spread throughout the coastal cities faster than a firestorm.

It is a delight to picture the effect Jesus' powerful sermon recorded in Matthew had on the crowds. People from every walk of life were crowded onto that hillside, holding their breath so they wouldn't miss one word spoken by His resonant voice:

> *"Therefore I say to you, do not worry about your life, what you will eat or what you will drink; nor about your body, what you will put on. Is not life more than food and the body more than clothing? Look at the birds of the air, for they neither sow nor reap nor gather into barns; yet your heavenly Father feeds them. Are you not of more value than they?*

"Which of you by worrying can add one cubit to his stature? So why do you worry about clothing? Consider the lilies of the field, how they grow: they neither toil nor spin; and yet I say to you that even Solomon in all his glory was not arrayed like one of these. Now if God so clothes the grass of the field, which today is, and tomorrow is thrown into the oven, will He not much more clothe you, O you of little faith?

"Therefore do not worry, saying, 'What shall we eat?' or 'What shall we drink?' or 'What shall we wear?' For after all these things the Gentiles [pagans] seek. For your heavenly Father knows that you need all these things. But seek first the kingdom of God and His righteousness, and all these things shall be added to you."

Matthew 6:25-33

In the entire Sermon on the Mount as recorded by Matthew, Jesus refers seventeen times to God the Father. That emphasis tells us that Christ was not trying to teach specifics or a code of rules and laws. Rather, Jesus was determined to lead mankind into an atmosphere of understanding—letting us all realize that there is Someone bigger than we are, able to live within us, who can take care of life's every need.

In his book *Sacred Quest: Discovering Spiritual Intimacy with God,* pastor and author Doug Banister wrote about the dynamic influence that Jesus' life and teaching has on us today:

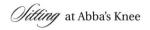

Talking, communicating, revealing, speaking, engaging, expressing, calling life into being—this is the essence of who Jesus is. Jesus said, "Man does not live by bread alone, but on every word that comes from the mouth of God."...Words are the bridges over which two people journey into relationship.... Words are equally important in our relationship with Jesus Christ. Jesus is the Word.... He is the expression of God's heart. He is the bridge over which we journey into relationship with God. He is the currency of our relationship with the Divine.[1]

Knowing Him means that my needs will be met. I don't have to worry anymore. If I grow like I'm supposed to, if I have a thriving relationship with my Father, then everything that I need I'll find in Him.

Jesus operated that way His whole life. When Jesus was just twelve years old, He sat at the temple in Jerusalem, engaging teachers and scholars in discussion about Scripture. His family packed up and left the city, and although they soon missed Him and came back looking for Him, He had became so caught up in the teaching of the Word of God that He didn't miss them. When Jesus' parents found Him, the first thing He said was "...Why did you seek Me? Did you not know that I must be about My Father's business?"[2]

For eighteen years after that, we don't hear anything about Jesus' life, and then suddenly His ministry bursts

onto the scene again. We find Him at the waters of the Jordan River, about to be baptized. As Jesus arose out of the water and the Holy Spirit hovered over Him in the form of a dove, the Father spoke and said, "...This is My beloved Son, in whom I am well pleased."[3]

At another time, the disciples went looking for Jesus, who had arisen early one morning. They found Him bowed earnestly in prayer, speaking to God as easily as a son speaks to a father. With yearning, they begged Him, "Lord, teach us to pray.[4] We want a relationship like that."

It is amazing to note that Jesus never did or said anything without the Father's permission. He says in the gospel of John, "What you see me doing, I've seen the Father do, and I'm doing what He does." He said, "The words that I say to you are not My words. They are what I've heard the Father say."[5]

Perhaps the greatest trial of Jesus' life was in the Garden of Gethsemane just before He was arrested. The Gospels record the incredible pressure that came upon Him in Gethsemane—capillaries broke and sweat and blood burst from His skin. But read closely—Mark's gospel records that the cry "Abba, Father!" came from His lips in His hour of agony.[6] In fact, that's the first mention of Abba in the New Testament. "Abba, Father...Take this cup away from Me; nevertheless, not what I will, but what You will."

Christ's faith in His Father didn't waver even as He was taken before Pilate for His trial. At one point Jesus calmly looked at Pilate and said, "Do you think that I cannot now pray to My Father, and He will provide Me with more than twelve legions [approximately 72,000] of angels?"[7]

When they nailed Him to a cross, the first thing Jesus said was, "...Father, forgive them; for they know not what they do...."[8] And His final words in that dark hour were, "...Father, into thy hands I commend my Spirit...."[9]

Three days later, Christ broke out of His tomb, released from the chains of death! Reassuring His disciples before His final return to heaven, He charged them to tarry in Jerusalem and wait for the promise of the Father.[10] He wasn't leaving them without hope—the Father had special provision for those who believed in Him.

The Father—Alive in Us

When you are embraced into the family of Abba God, there are things your heavenly Parent wants to do for you! It is not a list of rules to keep or a code to follow. This Father, who came to earth in the Person of Jesus Christ and then sent the Holy Spirit into you so that you would have Father guidance in your life, has His loving eyes fixed upon you.[11]

A Blazing Light

Your Father, Abba, wants you to shine! Jesus charged us strongly in Matthew 5:16, "Let your light so shine before men, that they may see your good works and glorify your Father in heaven." There is no room for dullness, for a tarnished life, in the hope He expresses for us! The same God who painted the world with magnificent bronze, green, blue, red, and yellow hues also has poured His Spirit into you so that you might shine, not with your own glory, but reflecting the brilliant glory of God.

Evangelist David Ring has had cerebral palsy for years, but his upbeat spirit and life of faith continue to inspire believers everywhere. One of his favorite statements is "Don't whine—shine!"

If you invited Jesus into your heart, your heavenly Father came into your life to put a glow in you, to light up your life, to put something in you that you didn't have, to cause you to burn and blaze with His glory in your life. (If you haven't received Jesus as your Lord and Savior and you would like to, there is a prayer you can pray at the end of this book.) No life is ordinary or dull that comes in contact with the power of Jesus Christ. The divine light can shine out through you. He can transform you with His power.

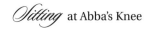

An Unending Love

Jesus gives more admonition in Matthew 6:6, "But you, when you pray, go into your room, and when you have shut your door, pray to your Father who is in the secret place; and your Father who sees in secret will reward you openly."

Your Father knows all your secrets and loves you anyway! It doesn't matter what you've thought, what you've done, or what places you've been that you are ashamed of. The Father has seen it all and loves you anyway.[12] His love and His grace cover all sin.[13] He knows the worst about you and still loves you. He knows your secrets, and He still loves you.

An Intimate Connection

Matthew 6:6 implies that God desires intimacy with you. Notice *The New King James Version* translates that verse as "...the secret place." In other words, God wants to invite you in, spiritually, to a place of intimacy with Him. Psalm 91:1 talks about it, saying, "He who dwells in the secret place of the Most High shall abide under the shadow of the Almighty."

The secret place is that place of private communion where your spirit and God's Spirit alone can talk to one another. It is a place where you can be in the center of His embrace,[14] where His caress can reach your spirit. It

is a place where He can love you, and you can love Him—in the secret place of the Most High.

When my son, Ronnie, was a senior in high school, he was preparing to go on a trip with friends of our family. He would be gone for several days, so the night before we sat together in his room and talked awhile. When I came out, my wife played the part of an FBI agent, quizzing me, "What did you all go into that room for?" She didn't know that Ronnie had told me earlier in the day that he wanted to see me alone.

That evening was special to me because of what we discussed. Of course, Ronnie being a teenager, one of the things we discussed was spending money for the trip! But in the course of our talking, he looked me in the eye and said, "Daddy, we need to spend some time together every day."

That touched me so deeply! I had already given him some money, so he wasn't trying to get something out of me. He said, "Daddy, we need to talk every day so we understand each other."

Nothing takes the place of time. You've got a Father who has time for you.

An Abundant Provision

Your heavenly Father knows your needs. We see evidence of that in Matthew 6:8 when Jesus declared,

"Your Father knows the things you have need of before you ask Him." But He still wants you to ask Him. One reason is that He wants to spend time with you. Maybe that's why we have shortages in our lives—because sometimes we have neglected to spend time with our Abba Father. Somehow, if we hit a shortage, we will show up in the secret place of prayer. Isn't that sad that we have to become desperate before we go into His Presence to talk to Him?

He is a Father who wants to lavish generously upon you everything you need. Remember Matthew 7:11: "If you then, being evil, know how to give good gifts to your children, how much more will your heavenly Father who is in heaven give good things to those who ask Him!" Your Father in heaven is lavishly generous. He gives good gifts to His children.

My family used to make fun of me. I've established a holiday tradition of going shopping on Christmas Eve. I'm surely not the only man in the world who has this pattern established! Usually I've already bought presents for everyone on my list, but there seems to be something in me that pushes me to get "just one more thing!" Even when my daughters were in college, I'd buy them a doll or something equally frivolous. There is something about being a father that makes you want to lavish something good on your children.

You've got a heavenly Father who wants to give you good things.

An Eternal Home

He's also a Father who wants you to go to heaven. Jesus laments in Matthew 7:22 KJV that when the judgment comes, not everyone who says to Him "Lord, Lord" shall enter the kingdom of heaven. God doesn't want anyone to perish, so He sent His Son to make the payment for the sins of all mankind.[15] It is each person's individual response to that payment that makes the difference.

One of my favorite authors has been a man named Brennan Manning. He used to be a Roman Catholic priest of the Franciscan order. He was filled with the Holy Spirit back in the 1970s. God brought him to a deeper level of truth, and he became a prolific teacher and writer, not just among Catholics, but among non-denominational groups all across the land.

Manning wrote a wonderful book called *Abba's Child: The Cry of the Heart for Intimate Belonging.*[16] In listening to some of his tapes, I learned that his birth name is not Brennan; his name is Richard Manning. That intrigued me, and I wanted to find out how he got the name Brennan. One thing I found out was that

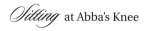

when you become a Catholic priest, you choose the name of a saint as a new name.

I soon discovered that his best friend was named Ray Brennan. He and Ray went off from Chicago to the Korean War together. One dark night in a supposedly dormant battle zone, they were sharing a chocolate bar, passing it back and forth, and sharing conversation. In seconds, the tranquility was shattered as a stray grenade fell into their foxhole. Without even thinking, Ray Brennan threw his body over that grenade and took the full impact of the explosion. The last thing he did was lift his head and smile and wink at his friend, Richard Manning, who at that point wasn't really right with the Lord. It was out of that experience that Richard found himself seeking God, compelled toward the high calling that was his.

The day came for Richard to be ordained, and they asked, "By what name do you wish to be called?" He said, "I want to be called Brennan, because Ray Brennan died for me. I want to carry his name."

I want to carry the name of my heavenly Father, because He allowed His Son Jesus to die for me, to fling His body on the grenade of judgment and take its explosion into His own body that I might cry, "Abba, Father" today. It is not about signing a set of rules, joining some religious organization, or conforming to traditions and church dictates. Do you think God

would allow His Son to come and be nailed to a bloody tree, to suffer the sting of a whip, just so you could be a part of some religious organization or establishment? No! He allowed His Son to die on the cross to take the full weight of our sin so that He could change our lives forever and transform us into His children.

Can you call Him Abba today? How can we do anything but surrender at the feet of the One who took the deathblow to His heart for us! Sitting at the Father's knee, we find everything we need to take care of us for eternity.

Chapter 13

The *Waiting* Father

It has been called the greatest short story ever written. Charles Spurgeon preached the story in his sermon entitled "Many Kisses for Returning Sinners...." Rembrandt used it as the subject of his magnificent painting "The Return of the Prodigal Son."

Jesus loved sinners, and His life on earth was dedicated to the task of showing sinners a way back to the Father, their Creator. Mankind seemed to prefer a life away from Father God, but Jesus knew the deep hunger of the human soul and knew that the power of the Father's love could transform any life.

A Timeless Love Story

This great parable of Jesus was recorded in Luke 15, beginning in verse 11.

Then He said: "A certain man had two sons.

"And the younger of them said to his father, 'Father, give me the portion of goods that falls to me.' So he divided to them his livelihood.

"And not many days after, the younger son gathered all together, journeyed to a far country, and there wasted his possessions with prodigal living.

"But when he had spent all, there arose a severe famine in the land, and he began to be in want.

"Then he went and joined himself to a citizen of that country, and he sent him into his fields to feed swine.

"And he would gladly have filled his stomach with the pods that the swine ate, and no one gave him anything."

This story struck a chord with those sitting at the feet of Jesus, but it is just as relevant a tale today. Running away still seems to be a popular answer to life's problems. Every year, at least 1.3 million teenagers end up on the streets.[1] Of that number, some are never seen again. Many runaways eventually become involved in high-risk destructive behavior, such as drug abuse, prostitution, or gang activity. We see their pictures on milk cartons, billboards, and in advertisements in the mall. Something convinced those runaways that anything was better than home. Something inside lied to them, telling them if they could just escape from the authority over them, then life would be better.

The biblical runaway in Jesus' parable bought into those lies and reaped the tragic results. The Prodigal Son's experience illustrates four consequences of living your life away from Abba's protection.

A Life of Selfishness

We read in Scripture that the young son said, "Father, give me...." Even though this boy was probably at least seventeen or eighteen years of age, in this selfish phrase you can picture him as a four-year-old with hands and face sticky with honey, reaching up saying, "Gimme, Gimme, Gimme!"

This boy seemed to harbor hardness in his character. Normally, Jewish sons would receive their inheritance at their father's death. But this son was saying, "Old man, I really wish you were dead already. But I don't want to wait around, so I want one-third of the inheritance that is mine, and I want it now!"

That same attitude pervades our modern culture. The mantra of the business world has become, "I'll get what I want even if I have to run over you. I'll lie. I'll scheme. I'll cheat. I'll even join a church if it makes me look good. I want what's mine."

Church members often show a similar selfishness: *Can I be comfortable? Where is my usual seat? Why should I help out in the nursery? Why should I practice*

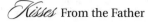

in the choir? Why should I teach a class? Why should I tithe? The pervading attitude is *What can the church do for me?*

The truth is that the church isn't here to do something for you. If you are saved, you *are* the church. You are the body of Christ. Though there are times that you will likely need to be ministered to, more often you must be willing to give of yourself to touch other members of the body. Living in the center of Abba's love forces you to push away a lifestyle of total selfishness.

Wasted Possessions

It is too simple a trap to waste time, character, talent, and even finances, pouring our lives into what doesn't really matter. I was astounded along with other television viewers in October of 1998, when I watched a retired prominent entomologist hold 109 live honey-bees in his closed mouth for ten seconds to break a world record![2] Since then he's continued his unsettling quest, beaten his own record several times, and been seen again recently on television sporting a body suit made up of over 200,000 bees!

I'm not going to try to beat him out of that record! My first thought was *What a way to be remembered—*

spending all of your life so history would record that you could hold more bees in your mouth than anybody else!

I once read of a man who won a big payout in the Delaware lottery, but in just a few short years from his big win, he was standing in bankruptcy court.

Before we get too judgmental, we must look inward and realize that we too often are guilty of squandering the investments of heaven that brought us into the world, that sustain us, that bring us joy. We have said, "Give me mine."

The Prodigal Son was also guilty of this. Luke 15:13 goes on to state that the son "wasted his possessions." The father handed over the bag of coins, and in a few days, the selfish son hit the road. In short order he blew all his money.

You could imagine this prodigal in the modern day, renting a nice office, investing in a business. Soon everybody hears that he has a bankroll, and he suddenly finds himself surrounded by friends. He buys a condo. He buys new clothes to get "the look." He is soon busy with appointments, going here and there. Business is important, but his social life becomes more and more his chief obsession. He is pouring his life into pleasure and enjoying every minute of it.

Then the tragic morning comes—he wakes to the news that his stocks have dropped through the floor. Everything he has risked is now gone. He calls his

banker friends and they say, "Your credit line has run out." In desperation, he looks around, but all his new friends are mysteriously "unavailable." Everything he owned has been blown to the wind. Gone. Bankrupt.

In the story of the Prodigal Son, one of the most astounding parts of the story is the fact that the father even granted the son's request for his inheritance in the first place! Would you actually write the check if your child walked up to you and said, "I'm tired of living with you. I don't like you. In fact, if you were dead, I'd be better off. Can I have a third of your money and get my inheritance now?" This father did hand over the money, even knowing that the son was likely too immature to handle that responsibility.

The Father has showered upon all of us blessings innumerable, some that we take for granted. For example, what if we had to pay for the very oxygen we breathe? How often do we fall into the cycle of obsessing about what we can't have instead of focusing upon the abundant blessings that God has specially poured into our lives! Satan will always point out that it looks better "over there," pointing out that one thing you can't have. If you live in your own understanding instead of on God's promises, you could throw your life away over that one thing and miss the blessing and destiny God has prepared for you.

A Life of Emptiness

A life away from Abba is also a life filled with void and want. Luke 15:14-16 describe how the Prodigal Son soon began to experience that kind of life, saying, "But when he had spent all, there arose a severe famine in that land, and he began to be in want. Then he went and joined himself to a citizen of that country, and he sent him into his fields to feed swine." The language used indicates that he was beginning to starve to death.

I am fairly certain that few people who will read this book have ever known true physical hunger. Other than abstaining before a medical test or a short-term fast, we can't say we've experienced the severe pain and gnawing hunger of being without food. This wayward son was so desperate for nourishment that even the food he was feeding the hogs began looking good to him.

More prevalent than physical hunger in this country is spiritual hunger. The emptiness often drives people into any spiritual experience that promises results. I have heard Christians say, "How can rational people ever find themselves involved in occult or New Age practices?" It comes down to a simple fact: If there is nothing on the table where you are, you will eat garbage to stay alive.

I'm not surprised at what people do. I'm not surprised at the alternative "spiritual tables" from

which they try to feed, especially when they come from churches that are dried up, dead, and empty, with nothing of substance except traditions and laws. People are looking for something real and sustaining. In a day of emptiness such as we live in, people need something from the Lord that is substantial and power-ful. Life away from the sustaining power of a Father God who cares is a life of emptiness.

A Life of Loneliness

One of the saddest statements in this parable is recorded in Luke 15:16: "...no one gave him anything." This wayward son had reached the lowest point of his life, and no one even cared.

The prodigal looked around and, no doubt, thought of the psalmist's words "Look on my right hand and see...no one cares for my soul."[3] This boy couldn't even get anybody to give him permission to eat the hog's swill. He was empty, and he was alone.

It is right at this point in a person's life, when something has gone wrong, when there has been a reversal, that the devil shows up with the most despair-ing of lies: "You can't get home from here."

That is what happened to this son. This boy, no doubt raised a devout Jew, had joined himself with a Gentile and worked as a keeper of hogs, animals that were unclean to him. The word used for "joined" in the Greek can also be translated "to glue."[4] This son felt locked into this partnership. He was overcome with despair at the lies the devil whispered to him: "You will never get out of this. You have blown it now. You can't get home from here. You might as well just end your life now. You are ruined."

However, these were all nothing but lies. There indeed was one who still loved the boy and had not given up! Scripture says that the father (Abba) stood on the porch, and when the boy was a great way off, he saw him. There had been many days that the boy had never thought of his father, but this daddy had never forgotten the son and held him close in his heart, even from a far country.

Then the day of awakening arrived. Luke wrote, "...he came to himself...." The son realized that even the servants in his father's house had things better than he did at that moment. He realized he had one last chance—go home and beg to be received by the one he had hurt.

The original Greek expression for "came to himself" indicates *to stand outside of your body.*[5] We get our idea of schizophrenia from the same expression. The boy had become someone else. He became something he was never intended to be, almost as if something else had been in control of his life. To live in sin, to live in

wrong, to live away from the Father—this is a decision rooted in insanity. He had been categorically insane.

But when he woke up, it was as if his spirit came back into him. All of a sudden he realized where he was and where he had landed, and he decided to go back to Abba's house. Who do you think it was that woke him up and brought him to himself? I believe it was the Holy Spirit! The boy made up his mind to go home, for the Comforter, the Holy Spirit, prompted this boy to recall the love of his father.

Helmut Thielicke, the brilliant German professor and theologian, wrote of the son's sudden awakening:

>...How did it come about that he suddenly broke away from the desert and the pigsty? Was it because it stank to high heaven? Was it because he had had enough of the farmer who gave him only husks to eat? Was it because he was sick and tired of his miserable standard of living? None of this would have driven him to make a break; he would probably have hanged himself and put an end to it in this way.
>
>But that he sprang to his feet and began to run, began to run home, to his father; that a feeling of strength swept through him and he became active—this was because suddenly the vision of his father's house loomed up in his soul and he saw in spirit the father waving and beckoning to him; and suddenly he knew and was sure that the father would accept

him if he went. Sure, he was fed up with the far country...But this was only incidental. The main thing was simply the joy of realizing: I can go home again![6]

In the lowest moment of your time away from the Father's house, the devil will accost you, saying, "You can't get home from here." Perhaps it is a religious, legalistic past that traps you. Or maybe it is a broken marriage, a failed ministry, or a poor decision that holds you in the bondage of fear and despair.

Maybe you are one who has been burned by religious types, and you say, "I tried church. I've seen too many hypocrites, and I said that I would never walk back into another church." But it is not the open doors of a church that beckon you; it is the loving, generous arms of Daddy God that await you. A blood-stained, empty cross, once nailed into the hill of Golgotha, is a symbol that states, "You can come home."

The story has been told of a sailor and two crew members who had the misfortune of having their ship damaged in a storm. Knowing land was miles away but seeing that their ship was about to sink, they jumped in the ocean to try to make it to land. The water was bitterly cold, and in a short amount of time, two of the crew died from the elements. However, the third sailor began to stroke for the shore. He swam for hours, seeing the shoreline in the distance.

Along the way, he began hearing a sinister voice whispering to him over the waves, "Why don't you stop and rest right here?" He was so tired that he almost stopped, but another voice floated to him from above, "Son, if you stop now, you will never get home. If you stop now, you will never get home." The voice gave him strength and courage, and he survived his bitter swim.

Can't you hear the Father saying that to you? If you stop and say, "Not me, I just can't go on through my pain and hardship," then your spiritual life will stagnate right where you are. You can get home from where you are. If a father could welcome home a swine-swill covered boy who stunk, how much more capable is Abba God of welcoming any struggling child into the haven of His arms!

Coming Home

It warms the heart to read the details of the homecoming of this poor, desolate son.

> *"But when he came to himself, he said, 'How many of my father's hired servants have bread enough and to spare, and I perish with hunger! I will arise and go to my father, and will say to him, "Father, I have sinned against heaven and before you, and I am no longer worthy to be called your son. Make me like one of your hired servants."'"*

"And he arose and came to his father. But when he was still a great way off, his father saw him and had compassion, and ran and fell on his neck and kissed him.

"And the son said to him, 'Father, I have sinned against heaven and in your sight, and am no longer worthy to be called your son.'

"But the father said to his servants, 'Bring out the best robe and put it on him, and put a ring on his hand and sandals on his feet. And bring the fatted calf here and kill it, and let us eat and be merry; for this my son was dead and is alive again; he was lost and is found.' And they began to be merry."

Luke 15:17-24

The Father's Watch

This father beheld his son with a gracious gaze. No matter how far the young man journeyed into darkness, he never got beyond the gracious gaze of his loving father. It was a long watch. The father could see how far down he had gone, and he still loved him. The father had waited a long time, and he was watching and ready for his son to return.

There is not one thing you can do to keep God from loving you! There is no pit so deep that His gracious gaze doesn't look upon you with mercy and compassion. There is no debt you have that He can't discharge.

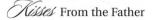

There is no failure He can't fix. There is no darkness He can't illuminate. No matter how deep in sin we fall, we're never so far away that the river of the blood of Jesus cannot wash the dirt away. Daddy God has a long watch on you! In fact, before the first wave crashed upon the first shore of this planet, He determined to put you on this planet and to love you.

The picture of this waiting father is so poignant. There he was, standing on the portico of his Middle Eastern home, looking down the road, when he saw a figure approaching. While the figure may have looked frail and bent over and dirtier than he had ever been before, there was an unmistakable mark of the father's image upon this approaching vision. The father immediately recognized him and knew that this was his beloved son!

Each believer holds an unmistakable mark of the Father's image upon one's life. Abba God can recognize you coming up the road. He can see you walking up that highway of repentance.

The Father's Welcome

What do you do with a repentant sinner? Our human nature is not prone to easy forgiveness, but God's love has no limits and knows no reserve in welcoming the wandering child home.

Jesus came to say, "Let me tell you how the Father welcomes someone home." Look at Luke 15:20. "...When he was still a great way off, his father saw him...and ran...." It was unheard of to see a Middle Eastern father run. It was undignified. The children would run to their father but not the father to the children, or in this case, to the son. Jesus shook up the religious crowd with the picture of a father running to a sinner.

The same verse says that the father "...fell on his neck...." You can see the boy almost trying to kneel when the father caught him under his arms and lifted him up. Face to face and eye to eye, he caressed that dirty face, ignored the unbrushed teeth, the matted hair, and torn clothes—it didn't matter to the father. He began to kiss his boy. In the Greek New Testament, it is in the present tense: "He kept on covering his face with kisses."[7]

How do you welcome a sinner home? The father threw a party, complete with dancing and music. The very idea of a watching, loving, running, dancing, kissing God insults some people's religion. But that is Abba Father!

The Father's Ways

The boy tried to confess his failure to his father, but in verse 22 the father told his servants, "...Bring forth

the best robe...." Just as the Scots have their tartan and the British their coats of arms, Jewish people of means in those days sometimes had a unique fabric woven just for their family, and sons and daughters got to wear the family garment.

Months before, most likely the boy had taken his ring off, the signet ring of the family. The ring was the equivalent of a credit card, letting him take part in family business.[8] He had taken off that family robe and left the protection of his father's house in selfishness. But after he left, I believe the father picked up that robe. You notice that the father didn't have to tell the servant where these items were.

No doubt when the son left the home, the father carefully placed the robe and the ring in a special place and could have said to his servants, "Put a new pair of shoes here too. He'll be back." And when the boy returned, he was joyfully wrapped in that clean family robe, representing his acceptance, and given back the signet ring, representing his authority restored.

There came a day when the Lord Jesus Christ wrapped a robe of His righteousness around my dirty soul, washing me in the blood of Calvary! He gave me the signet ring of authority, allowing me victory over the devil and his evil forces. He put the gospel shoes of peace upon my feet, making me walk differently.

I was reminded of this a couple years ago after holding a crusade meeting in the church of one of my preacher friends. I returned to my office, and in the mail was a box containing a beautiful pair of deerskin shoes! I had just shown my wife, Paulette, the worn-out soles of my dress shoes as I had packed for the crusade, and apparently one of the church members there had noticed them also. Inside was a short note: "How beautiful on the mountain are the feet of them that preach the Gospel."[9]

Those shoes truly feel good on my feet, but I'll tell you about a better pair! Calvary provided a pair of shoes that allows me to spread peace and hope to the world! And they are available to all who run to the Father's embrace.

The Church's Call to the World

The body of Christ spends a lot of time in the church doing our voting and issuing our edicts. We are saying to a lost world, "Go and do as you please; we have church business to take care of!" But the Father wants us to tell them He is saying, "Come home. Come home. I've been waiting for you. I've been watching for you. You were trapped in a lifestyle that has nearly destroyed you, but come home now. I'll clean you up. I'll put a robe on you. I'll fill you with the Holy Spirit. Come home."

A story has circulated on the Internet, and while its validity is difficult to verify, it so completely represents our human tendency to reject the unlovely. As the story goes, a young veteran in the Vietnam crisis was on his way home to his parents. He landed in San Francisco and phoned them, saying, "I'm here."

They joyfully said, "Great! Come on home."

He said, "I'm bringing a friend."

They said, "Fine."

The boy cleared his throat, "Well, Mom, Dad—you need to understand that he has lost an arm and a leg."

Suddenly the parents became uncomfortable, "Well, Son, maybe it is best not to bring him. Somebody else can take care of him."

They awaited their son's arrival, but he never came. Three days later they received a call that it was believed their son had committed suicide. They had to go to San Francisco to identify the body. When they arrived, the coroner prepared them, "Now, of course, you know that this boy came home from Vietnam having lost an arm and a leg."

Stricken, they realized it was their own son who wanted to come home and had tried to test them to feel out their welcome of his mangled condition.

Thankfully, we have a Father whose welcome is complete, who loves the unlovely, who stands with open arms no matter our failure or crisis.

My prayer for you as you read this chapter echoes that prayed by Charles Spurgeon in his sermon on the Prodigal, preached in 1891:

> Lord, give to many poor trembling souls the will to come to Thee! Bring many sinners to Thy blessed feet, and while they are yet a great way off, run and meet them; fall on their neck, give them many kisses of love, and fill them to the full with heavenly delight, for Jesus Christ's sake! Amen.[10]

SECTION FOUR

The *Vision* of the *Father*

Chapter 14

Abba's Story: *Hug* of a Second Chance

The group of believers filled the room, shoulder to shoulder.[1] Some sat on tables, feet dangling in front of the faces of children and infants who had settled in under the sturdy furniture for quiet play. Adults shifted and readied themselves to hear the apostle speak of Yeshua and the Father's love one more time.

The apostle scanned the faces of those in attendance and was struck by the sense of raw hunger and longing in their expressions. The eyes looked careworn, discouraged, and confused. *So much like sheep,* he thought. And suddenly he knew that tonight he must share the story he had long withheld about one of his last conversations with Yeshua. For after all, it was time they knew the Father had given him a second chance. Even as he began to speak and the room became quiet, that past rushed over him as though it had been yesterday, and Peter was gripped with emotion.

Unconditional Love

Never had the night felt so cold. Peter had stumbled blindly along the dark path toward the high priest's courtyard, keeping a safe distance behind the mob that had dragged his Master from Gethsemane. Now he stood shivering inside the courtyard gate, and his mind whirled with questions. "Why the Master? Why now? He said His kingdom was coming! What is happening? What are we to do now?"

A young servant girl with a saucy face stopped next to him, peering at him in the hazy light of the coal fire nearby. "Aren't you one of that Man's disciples?" she blurted.

His insides recoiled in fear. Managing a calm expression, he said, "I am not" and turned to warm his numb hands at the fire. His heart raced in panic and confusion, and his mind screamed, *What made me say that?*

Moments later he again felt a gaze upon him, and an accusing voice questioned, "You there, you're with that Yeshua, aren't you?" Emphatically, Peter said, "I'm not, I tell you!"

He retreated from the fire a bit, hoping the light would hide his face and keep the stares from lingering on him. But in a short time, he sensed a small group of men watching him across the courtyard. One of the

men finally crossed by the fire and stood in front of him. "You are one of those with that Yeshua," the fellow snarled, "for you are a Galilean, and your voice gives you away!"

Rage and fear overwhelmed Peter, and curse words poured from his lips loudly as he exclaimed, "I don't even know the Man you're talking about!"

And then time stood still for a moment.

The far-off crow of a rooster floated across the cold night. In agony, he recalled the Master's words the evening before, "Peter, before the rooster crows twice, you will deny me three times."

Bitter tears filled his eyes, and he ran.

He ran as the trial came to a close and Yeshua was beaten and ridiculed.

He ran as the Master was paraded through the narrow city streets and was forced to carry the heavy Roman cross on His bleeding back.

He ran as others stood vigil at the foot of the cross, watching the suffering of the One who had spent day and night with them for three years.

Then, when the Master gasped His last painful breath, and as His body was taken to a nearby borrowed tomb, Peter hid, alone and guilt-ridden, his tears his only sustenance.

Three days of hiding. Three days of fear. Three days of unrelenting floods of painful emotion. Peter finally joined the group of mourning disciples who were huddled together behind the locked doors of the weaver's shop, holding their breath each time they heard the cadence of a Roman battalion marching by.

Most of them were still asleep early on Sunday morning when the women began pounding on the outer door of the shop. And most of them scoffed as the women stumbled over their excited words, saying that the tomb was opened, exclaiming that Yeshua was alive and that angels at the tomb had said so. Mary Magdalene insisted it was true, so Peter motioned to John and they ran through the dim light of morning to the site of His burial.

John froze as they came to the open door of the Master's grave, but Peter, shaking, stepped within and saw the linen clothes folded in a neat pile. Peter could barely think, couldn't comprehend what this could mean. Turning, he and John retreated to the city.

Taking care to avoid the main streets, the disciples gathered late that same evening and exchanged the latest news—Mary claimed to have seen Him! In hushed tones, they debated what to think of her story. In addition, the Jewish council was in an uproar about the disappearance of the body, and word was out that the Master's followers were being sought out for questioning.

Suddenly, He was there before them! "Peace be to you," Yeshua had said.

Terror overcame them, as they thought He was a ghost or spirit. But as He gently reassured them, they calmed down and began to gather around Him, expressing their joy at His return and responding to His words of encouragement and instruction. Peter hovered near with the rest, but his heart was heavy. *I failed Him,* he thought. *I have no right to be by His side again.*

The days to follow were a blur to Peter, as he lived a confusing mix of restlessness, hope, and despondency. One morning he awoke and strolled down by the Sea of Tiberias. His fishing boat sat forlorn and empty, its nets bobbing to an enticing rhythm. In a sudden burst of resolve, Peter waded out to the boat. "Come join me!" he called to some of the disciples who appeared on the lakeside. "I'm going fishing!"

The familiar roughness of the rope, the lapping of the waves against the wooden planks, the hot sun beating on his back as he worked the nets—it all worked together to soothe some of the void in his heart. But as day turned to night and then to day again, they had caught nothing.

As the sun began to rise in the morning sky, Peter sat grumbling to himself, having checked the drooping nets for the hundredth time. He suddenly saw a figure beckon to them from the shore. "Children, don't you

have any food yet? Try casting your nets on the other side of the boat!"

Too tired to take the meddling stranger to task, Peter lifted the nets and shifted them quickly to the right side of the vessel. In moments, the boat began to list fearfully, and the fishermen leaned over to see the nets writhing with silver fins and tails. John pointed to the stranger on the shore. "It is the Lord!" he exclaimed.

Peter turned from the miraculous catch and fixed his eyes on Yeshua. Even across the water, he could sense the Master's steady gaze upon him. *He still wants me!* he realized. *He did this for me!*

In reckless abandon, Peter plunged into the water and swam for shore. When the boat drew to land, Yeshua said, "Bring some of the fish to the fire I've made here," and Peter dragged the bulging net ashore with the eagerness of a child wishing to please a father.

After they had all eaten their breakfast, most of the fishermen hurried to the boat to take care of the morning's catch, but Peter sat close by Yeshua in an awkward silence. The Master turned to him.

"Simon, do you love me more than these?"

Peter swallowed hard. Fear washed over him again, as he thought how unworthy he was to follow the Master. "Yes, Lord, you know I have affection for you."

The Master studied his face. "Feed My lambs."

The disciple sat silently—to think that the Master would call him to be a leader after what he had done! Then the Master spoke again.

"Simon, do you love me?"

Peter quickly replied, "Yes, Lord—You know I have affection for You!"

Yeshua said, "Tend to My sheep."

Peter looked at the hillside across the lake, watching some shepherds herding their flock toward higher pastures. Was he prepared for the task of leading others to walk in the way of Yeshua, when he himself failed to be strong in the Master's darkest hour?

Yeshua leaned forward and met Peter's eyes. "Simon, do you even have affection for Me?"

Tears filled Peter's eyes, and his heart twisted in grief, "Yeshua—you know everything there is to know. You know that I truly love You!"

The Master gripped him with His powerful gaze. "Simon, feed My sheep. When you were young, you made your own decisions and went where you pleased. But the time has come to follow Me."

More Than Enough Mercy

When Peter finished the story, he lifted a shaking hand, wiping away the tears that had streaked his face

as he shared with the small group of believers. Looking around, he saw many who wept openly.

"Be encouraged, children!" said the apostle, his voice thick with emotion as he arose to give his final charge of the evening. "Lay aside the things that hold you back. As newborn infants, seek after the pure milk of His Word so you can grow!"

He smiled and his voice grew strong. "I have tasted that the Lord is gracious—His own blood redeemed me and covered my failures. Call upon the Father for your every failure, every need. You will indeed find His mercy complete."

Oh, how I love that story because it is so relevant to us who believe today! You may feel that your life is filled with failure, that you've not walked in godliness and you've run from God's voice. Abba is waiting to assure you and nurture you—He is the God of the second chance. Don't be afraid to turn back to Him; His mercy is more than enough for you.

Chapter 15

Abiding in
Abba's House

Our Lord Jesus walked on this earth as a model of the Father. As we have observed often throughout this book, all of Jesus' actions were based upon what He saw the Father doing!

It is no mistake that God described the New Testament church as "the body of Christ."[1] The collective members of the church are in vital union with each other; the very life of the church depends upon this unity. When the church stands up in full unity and maturity, a watching world should see the heavenly Father clearly—it should be Abba's house!

The idea of the church having a front porch where a nurturing, loving Father stands waiting is not what the world thinks of Christianity. Instead, their impressions of Christian houses of worship are based upon what they see at first glance. And this is no fault of their

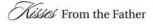

vision! Too often churches that have other agendas obscure the Father image of God.

The Courthouse

Some churches become known more for what they oppose than what they support! These churches usually have a more reactive than proactive stance on issues.

In my years of ministry, I realized that some churches hold creeds that are cultural, not biblical! As a lad in middle school and high school, the big issues tackled by the church crowd were dancing, slacks on girls, shorts, and hair length for boys. In the Southern churches, these external things were the righteous standards that made us Christians. Preachers staunchly admonished women to avoid wearing "that which pertains to a man." Churches split and pagans laughed over groups whose major focus was on this and other trivial codes.

Today when I reflect upon the trivia that was debated in our churches in those years, I am appalled. While we should have been engaging the critical issues of the time, such as civil rights, poverty, the fatherless, and other injustices around the globe, the evangelical world was arguing over hair length!

In Scripture, the book of Galatians confronts cultural and legalistic substitutes for real Christianity.

O foolish Galatians! Who has bewitched you that you should not obey the truth, before whose eyes Jesus Christ was clearly portrayed among you as crucified?

This only I want to learn from you: Did you receive the Spirit by the works of the law, or by the hearing of faith? Are you so foolish? Having begun in the Spirit, are you now being made perfect by the flesh? Have you suffered so many things in vain—if indeed it was in vain?

Therefore He who supplies the Spirit to you and works miracles among you, does He do it by the works of the law, or by the hearing of faith?—

Galatians 3:1-5

The message of the church should not be the witchcraft of legalism. Faith and the Holy Spirit are the secrets to a liberated, powerful church. The "Courthouse" church will not point the lost to a loving, waiting Father!

The Country Club

In the early 1990s, an affluent suburban church in a large Southern city was beginning a pastoral search. Asking my help, they gave me an overview of their church ministry. They were so proud of their state-of-the-art "wellness center." This multimillion-dollar structure provided all the benefits of an expensive spa. "Over 50,000 passed through our center last year," they bragged.

Excited to see their aggressive stance to serve their community, I asked eagerly, "Of those people, how many were given a witness about Jesus and how many came away with changed lives?"

They looked at me with a puzzled expression and answered a startling "None." Then in a deferring manner, they stated, "Pastor, you see, evangelism is not our 'style' or priority here."

It is possible in suburbia to grow a church on the basis of programs, activities, fitness centers, and special events. Some affluent churches become "the place to be" for all the "right people." This type of church echoes the model of the Laodician church mentioned in Revelation:

> "...you are lukewarm, and neither cold nor hot....you say, 'I am rich, have become wealthy, and have need of nothing'—and do not know that you are wretched, miserable, poor, blind, and naked—."
>
> Revelation 3:16,17

The Museum

The "Museum" type of church is the church that is modeling great traditionalism. This church has a great history and thrives on memories of the past. These churches boast a great heritage. They are often well-endowed financially and are eager to display

commemorative signs on every pew, window, and door front recognizing the donors of the past.

A word of balance is in order—churches must, of course, have financial means to undergird their ministry and work. God promises great blessings to those who give generously and with a joyful heart to support His work. However, the sole mission of the museum church is to preserve the past at all costs. Engaging a dying world is not the issue. Escaping the world through a nostalgic atmosphere of "the way things always have been" is how these churches stop their ears to the death rattles of a desperate, lost sea of humanity.

The church at Sardis was examined and pronounced dead by Jesus even though they still had "a name."

> *"And to the angel of the church in Sardis write, 'These things says He who has the seven Spirits of God and the seven stars: "I know your works, that you have a name that you are alive, but you are dead. Be watchful, and strengthen the things which remain, that are ready to die, for I have not found your works perfect before God."*
>
> Revelation 3:1,2

The Think Tank

This model of the church is popular today. We call it a teaching church. Everyone in the congregation has a notebook and can give you the meaning of the

important Greek and Hebrew words used in a sermon. The Word is taught and studied and great pride is taken in their knowledge. The Bible and in-depth commentaries, outlines, and studies become the goal instead of an encounter with the living Christ.

While we are carefully instructed to study to show ourselves approved unto God,[2] we must note the danger of replacing our intimacy with Abba with head knowledge.

> *"You search the Scriptures, for in them you think you have eternal life; and these are they which testify of Me. But you are not willing to come to Me that you may have life."*
>
> John 5:39,40

The Pharisees knew the Scriptures but missed the living Christ. They were always on the prowl, trying to trap Jesus in tricky, religious questions. We read of one attempt in Matthew 22:29, but Jesus' response showed He knew their hearts: "...You are mistaken, not knowing the Scriptures nor the power of God." Jesus let them know that scriptural information is not scriptural knowledge.

Of course, truly effective churches must diligently study the Scriptures. Bible study confirms the present work of Christ and draws us into a personal intimacy with Him. However, Bible study can become an idol in itself. The church's task is to teach Scripture in such a way that the holiness of the living God confronts the

individual. Unfortunately, some churches hold a reverence for intellect and learning that supersedes obedience to the Holy Spirit.

The Night Club

Some see the church as an entertainment center. Those on the platform are performing before an audience of people. Services must sparkle and shine with entertainment value or there is a fear we cannot keep our audience. This model can be enjoyable and attractive, drawing thousands, and yet, perhaps not one life is changed. The worship staff is under constant pressure to "top" the last spectacular performance!

A balance is in order, however. I cannot emphasize enough that the story we have to share is the best news the world will ever hear. It deserves to be told, whether in sermon, song, drama, or media, with excellence! Yet the message of the Cross, the description of Abba God, and the charge to His children must be clearly understood. The clear message will ensure that the church will stand boldly in Christ, "...and the gates of hell shall not prevail against it."[3]

The Mental Health Facility

In this picture, the church is a mental health facility that must take on the responsibility to heal the

personal needs of others. Counseling replaces the preaching of the Cross. While counseling is a true spiritual gift and one that edifies believers, some churches tap into modern psychology and, therefore, fail to use real truth to set people free.

In the "Mental Health Facility" church model, the awful reality of guilt from sin and the healing effects of true repentance are likely glossed over. The dark world of demons is discounted. The church member is advised, counseled, and referred to specialists and support programs, but seldom healed. Fleshly wisdom is leaned upon instead of the truth of spiritual warfare and healing. Counselors seem to forget "how God anointed Jesus of Nazareth with the Holy Spirit and with power, who went about doing good and healing all who were oppressed by the devil, for God was with Him."[4]

A Model To Follow: Abba's House

Jesus' ministry brought deliverance and help to the people of His day. We must recover the model of the church as the "household of God." Jesus came to bring us home to a Father who will forever love us and sustain us!

Now, therefore, you are no longer strangers and foreigners, but fellow citizens with the saints and

members of the household of God, having been built on the foundation of the apostles and prophets, Jesus Christ Himself being the chief corner stone.

Ephesians 2:19,20

When we first joined God's family, we became related to a worldwide family that stretches beyond time. We are standing on the sure foundation of Christ. We have a place where we can fit in, where we can keep growing, where we can experience the power of the Holy Spirit.

God has promised a corporate anointing, a powerful release of His own Presence when the church stands in unity.[5] After this unity forms, we are promised His grace, which manifests in the life-enriching gifts of the Spirit.[6] The creative form of Abba Himself is released when we all together pray "Our Father...."

Abba's house must be on the lookout for sinners. Some of them are coming into the church sanctuaries wearing biker's clothes. Some of them are going to have earrings, nose rings, and hairstyles of every sort when they show up. Some will come in with three-piece suits and gold and diamond jewelry. The Father has what each of them needs. Churches need to wake up and realize that we are the children of a loving and accepting Father. He is our Father, and He cares about the world.

The church is not a courthouse, a country club, a museum, a think tank, a nightclub, or a mental health facility. The church is Abba's house—a place of welcome, of worship, and of warmth to all who come.

Chapter 16

Forever in Abba's Arms

In the science fiction film *E.T. the Extra-Terrestrial*, audiences encounter a lovable little alien with extraordinary powers. E.T. does not belong on this planet, and only a few people even care how he feels—lonely, lost, confused. Perhaps the most poignant scene occurs when this child-like creature points his finger skyward and says, "Home." No matter how nice the circumstances he encounters, this world is not home to E.T.

In a strange way, that is true for us all. There is something in all of us that cannot accept a six-foot hole in the ground as our destiny. The writer of Ecclesiastes said, "...He has put eternity in their hearts...."[1] There are times that we all want to point a finger skyward and cry out "Home!"

A Place Called Home

The natural process of aging reminds us that this shell of a body we live in is temporary and fragile.

Somehow we never see ourselves quite as old as others. My own grandfather was in a rest home at age seventy-five. I went by to see him one time and asked, "Papa, is everything all right?" He responded, "Yes, I am fine," and then emphatically gesturing to his roommate, he exclaimed, "But that old man is driving me crazy!" Ironically, the roommate was younger than my grandfather!

The failure of our own family structures reminds us that there is another home with more permanent relationships. Try as we will, our family structures often shatter. Our Lord Jesus would have to die and be raised from the dead before His own earthly family would believe in Him. Today, with divorce and abuse at all-time highs, we need someplace to call home.

The difficulties of life also summon us homeward. The crime, disease, and heartache of this planet make us weary. The promise of a better world gives us hope.

One day we will go home! Jesus said it in John 14:19: "...Because I live, you will live also."

In Hebrews 12:9 Yahweh is called "...the Father of spirits...." When we drop away the body of this death, the last remnant of Adam's curse, Yahweh is the Father of our spirit. As Father, He will perform what He has promised. Consider once again the comfort of Romans 8:9-17 and 23:

But you are not in the flesh but in the Spirit, if indeed the Spirit of God dwells in you. Now if anyone does not have the Spirit of Christ, he is not His.

And if Christ is in you, the body is dead because of sin, but the Spirit is life because of righteousness.

But if the Spirit of Him who raised Jesus from the dead dwells in you, He who raised Christ from the dead will also give life to your mortal bodies through His Spirit who dwells in you.

Therefore, brethren, we are debtors—not to the flesh, to live according to the flesh. For if you live according to the flesh you will die; but if by the Spirit you put to death the deeds of the body, you will live.

For as many as are led by the Spirit of God, these are sons of God.

For you did not receive the spirit of bondage again to fear, but you received the Spirit of adoption by whom we cry out, "Abba, Father."

The Spirit Himself bears witness with our spirit that we are children of God,

and if children, then heirs—heirs of God and joint heirs with Christ, if indeed we suffer with Him, that we may also be glorified together.

Not only that, but we also who have the firstfruits of the Spirit, even we ourselves groan within ourselves, eagerly waiting for the adoption, the redemption of our body.

Here are the clear promises of God. First, the Holy Spirit's Presence is my mark of sonship. Second, the Holy Spirit will raise my dead body and make it immortal. Third, the Holy Spirit sets me free from the fear of death and its bondage. Fourth, the adoption into God's family is the resurrection of my body!

You and I are "born" into God's family at the new birth (when we receive Jesus as our Savior),[2] but we enter by adoption at the resurrection.[3] Adoption laws in Judaism and Roman law could never be reversed. The adopted child could never be disowned or robbed of any inheritance in the family. Thus, the fifth promise is a full inheritance in eternity.

A Glimpse of Heaven

"Home" for all eternity will one day be a reality! What will it be like in that day? While God is willing and able to heal, Ecclesiastes 3:2 says that there is a time to live and a time to die. Having stood by the bedsides of many at the time of their death, I think I have caught a hint of the reality of that day.

First, I believe that angels will escort us home. Once I stood by the hospital bed of a dying child while the family stood outside the room. All of a sudden standing at the head of the bed was a figure clad in white. In the

dim light of the hospital room, I assumed that it was one of the medical personnel.

I looked up at this tall person and heard his deep voice say, "She will soon be fine." I immediately stepped outside the room to give what I thought was a hopeful prognosis from a doctor. The family looked at me incredulously and said, "Pastor, there was no one in the room but you!" We stepped back in the room and the person was gone, along with the spirit of the beloved family member. An angel had come to take her home to her Father.

On another occasion, I stood by the bed of a dying minister who was quite old. All day long before he passed on to glory, he kept singing, "O come, angel band, come and around me stand, O bear me away on your golden wings to my immortal home."

At our darkest moments we must remember "Home!" Isaiah 9:6 called Yahweh our "everlasting Father." One of the Hebrew words for "everlasting" is "eternity,"[4] which means that "everlasting Father" could be translated "Father of Eternity." Abba will never die, nor will He ever forsake us.

Second, we will have a place to live in heaven! I love what Jesus said to His disciples shortly before He went away. We find the word recorded in John 14:1-4,18 and 19. In this marvelous passage, Jesus promises us a place in the Father's house! The phrase "In my Father's house

are many mansions..." could be translated, "In my Father's house are many rooms" or "apartments," the emphasis being on family, not luxury. We live together with Him under His care.

In this season in which we live now, remember His promise, "I will not leave you orphans...." In the meantime, in this age of "not yet," we have the Holy Spirit crying "Abba Father" as a comfort to us.

Third, at death we see the Lord! The Bible says, "...to be absent from the body" is "to be present with the Lord."[5] You see, "...The Lord our God is one Lord."[6] We will see Jesus, who is our Father as well.

Heaven is described beautifully in Revelation 21 as a city of gold and jewels, a fair city, a country, and our inheritance. What really makes heaven beautiful and what lights its atmosphere is Jesus. I love the verse that rejoices, "They shall see His face...."[7]

One of the great writers of hymns, Fanny Crosby, was blind. That fact makes one particular hymn that she wrote all the more touching to the listener.

> When my life work is ended, and I cross the
>   swelling tide,
> And the bright and glorious morning I shall see;
> I shall know my Redeemer when I reach the
>   other side,
> And His smile shall be the first to welcome me.

I shall know Him, I shall know Him,
And redeemed by His side I shall stand,
I shall know Him, I shall know Him,
By the prints of the nails in His hand.[8]

Finally, we are promised a brand-new body! There shall be a resurrection, and we shall live in a new body that is not subject to age, disease, or death![9]

Some years ago, I suffered what the doctors called a "heart incident." My heart stopped suddenly, and I fainted. I remember the sensation of weightlessly moving across a field of wild flowers, speeding toward a group of brightly shining individuals. I thought I heard music like the sound of a symphony mixing with the rushing roar of waterfalls.

As I moved toward the crowd waiting for me, I suddenly heard a voice far across the field calling me, "Daddy, Daddy!" With a jolt I found myself conscious again with my daughter, Kelli, crying over me and calling my name.

Of course, my brush with eternity made me think about what the passage there would be like. For a few moments, I felt the wind of eternity on my face, inhaled a deathless atmosphere, saw flowers that bloom forever, and heard celestial music. I do not know all that awaits us, but I believe there is a welcome party prepared for us. I am sure Abba stands waiting for His children.

My First Five Minutes in Heaven

Not long ago, a close friend asked me, "Ron, what will it be like when I get to heaven?"

I began to recite the usual clichés drawn from the biblical descriptions of mansions, streets of gold, and gates of pearl. He interrupted me, "No, no," he urged. "I mean, what will it be like when I first get there? Who will welcome me? How will I know what to do?"

I don't know that I gave him a satisfactory answer, but I have since thought a great deal about what it will be like during those first five minutes in heaven. I think my friend hit on the key question, wondering what kinds of relationships we will enjoy and if we'd be ready.

I found my answer hidden away in the little letter of 2 Peter 1:11: "for so an entrance will be supplied to you abundantly into the everlasting kingdom of our Lord and Savior Jesus Christ."

Digging into the word meanings in this verse paints for us a beautiful picture of how God prepares for our entrance into heaven. One of the translations of the word *supplied* comes from a Greek word that is the basis for our modern word "choreographed."[10] A chore-ographer makes sure every step and every movement of the chorus is right. At one time this person tradition-ally was responsible for meals, lodging, costumes, and other supplies for the group he oversaw.

How fitting that "supplied" is used in 2 Peter 1:11 to describe the believer's entrance into eternity! The word indicates that *all* needs are thought of and met in abundance.[11] The root of this Greek word is also found in the passage about the Prodigal Son. It described the dancing that occurred when the wayward son returned home. It indicates that the joyful father hired an orchestra and choreographed the celebration to provide all that was needed for this special welcome home party.

I thought of this word and reflected more on my entrance into eternity. During my first five minutes in heaven, my first overwhelming desire will be to love and adore my Abba. I will know my Abba, Jesus, and He will know me! Abba will have choreographed my welcome; music will swell through the perfect atmosphere. Joy will be exhibited in the dance of eternal life. Angels will look on in wonder and amazement. I will instantly have fullness of knowledge. Long ago, the Holy Spirit was deposited in my heart as a down payment of the future. Now faith will become sight as I take up residence in a world free of all limits.

In heaven, I will find that time will no longer matter. Health will no longer be an issue. Death will be past history! Distance will not exist. Relationships will be enriched, crossing over the barriers that plagued us on earth. Moses, Esther, David, Ruth, Peter, Paul, and

other biblical figures will become as real and as dear to us as the friends we've known on earth.

And that reminds me: I will also see my loved ones who went on to heaven before me! My Dad and I will embrace forever. Best of all, we will see Jesus. Remember, "...to be absent from the body" is "to be present with the Lord."[13]

In these sublime truths, I rest my hope. My destiny is not to be eternal nothingness in an ornate box buried six feet in the ground. My future is the lap of God, who has told me to call Him Daddy!

Endnotes

Introduction

1 Mark 14:36.

2 Romans 8:15.

3 Galatians 4:6.

4 *New Unger's Bible Dictionary* originally published by Moody Press of Chicago, Illinois. Copyright © 1988, s.v. "ABBA." Used by permission.

5 W. E. Vine, *Expository Dictionary of New Testament Words* (Old Tappan, New Jersey: Fleming H. Revell Company, 1966), p. 9, s.v. "ABBA."

Chapter 1

1 Tommy Barnett, ed., *The Spirit of Christmas: Celebrating a Spirit-Filled Holiday Season* (Nashville: Thomas Nelson, 1999), from the sermon "Call Him Wonderful" by contributing author Dr. Ron Phillips, pp. 32-34.

2 Jonathan Rauch, "The Widening Marriage Gap: America's New Class Divide," *National Journal, The Atlantic Online* (May 23, 2001). Available from <http://www.theatlantic.com/politics/nj/rauch2001-05-23.htm.>

Chapter 2

1 Charles Hadden Spurgeon, *Morning and Evening* (Grand Rapids: Zondervan, reprint 1980), entry: "Morning, January 26, 'Your heavenly Father.'"

2 Luke 19:10.

3 John 14:9.

4 John 14:18.

5 John 14:16,17.

6 Vine, Vol. IV. SET-Z, p. 235, s.v. "WORSHIP, WORSHIPPING, A. Verbs, 1. PROSKUNEO."

7 See Luke 15:20.

8 Exodus 4:22.

9 "The youngest are commonly the fondlings of the family, but, it should seem, David was least set by of all the sons of Jesse; either

they did not discern or did not duly value the excellent spirit he was of." *Matthew Henry's Commentary on the Whole Bible: New Modern Edition* (Electronic Database: Hendrickson Publishers, Inc., copyright © 1991), s.v. "1 Samuel 16:6-13, David anointed by Samuel."

[10] Because of Saul's jealousy toward David, he tried to kill David several times.

[11] Psalm 103:13.

[12] Isaiah 63:16.

[13] Malachi 2:10.

[14] See Job 38:7.

[15] See James 1:17.

[16] See Hebrews 12:9.

[17] See 1 Corinthians 8:6.

Chapter 3

[1] This chapter contains the author's paraphrased narrative of the story of Adam and Eve in the Garden of Eden and their fall when they listened to the serpent and ate the fruit of the forbidden tree. It is found in the book of Genesis, chapters 1, 2, and 3.

[2] See Isaiah 14:12.

[3] See Luke 10:18.

[4] See John 8:44.

Chapter 4

[1] Genesis 12:3.

[2] Romans 4:11,12,16-18.

[3] Based on a definition from Thayer and Smith, *The KJV New Testament Greek Lexicon,* "Greek Lexicon entry for Doxa," entry #1391, s.v., "glory," available from <http://www.biblestudytools.net/Lexicons>.

[4] Donald W. Osgood, *Fatherbond* (Wheaton, Illinois: Tyndale House, 1989), p. 23.

[5] See Exodus 33:21-23.

[6] See Genesis 16:2.

[7] See Genesis 16:15.

[8] See Genesis 16:9,10 TLB.

[9] See Genesis 25:1,2.

[10] Based on a definition from James Strong, "Hebrew and Chaldee Dictionary" in *Strong's Exhaustive Concordance of the Bible* (Nashville: Abingdon, 1890), p. 49, entry #3173, s.v. "thy son," Genesis 22:2.

[11] Arthur Pink, *Gleanings in Genesis* (Chicago: Moody Bible Institute, 1922), p. 224.

[12] "...we must not suppose that this was the language merely of faith and obedience, the patriarch spoke prophetically, and referred to that Lamb of God which HE had provided for himself, who in the fullness of time should take away the sin of the world, and of whom Isaac was a most expressive type...." *Clarke's Commentary*, by Adam Clarke, Electronic Database (Biblesoft, 1996), s.v. "Genesis 22:8."

[13] Matthew 3:17.

[14] John 3:16.

Chapter 5

[1] 1 Peter 1:8.

[2] Nehemiah 8:10.

[3] Genesis 17:18,19.

[4] See Psalm 30:11.

[5] See Isaiah 61:3.

[6] Matthew 5:3-11.

[7] Matthew 27:46.

[8] Strong, "Hebrew and Chaldee Dictionary," p. 75, entry #5027, s.v. "look," Habakkuk 1:13.

[9] Matthew 3:17.

[10] See Matthew 27:59,60.

[11] See 1 Thessalonians 5:9.

[12] See Genesis 24.

[13] See Genesis 26:23-33.

[14] Isaiah 54:7,8.

[15] See Psalm 103:12.

[16] See Psalm 23:6.

Chapter 6

1 Romans 8:6.

2 God often deals with us through conviction (never condemnation) by showing us our faults, like wrong attitudes and actions. When we face the truths He reveals to us, He helps us to overcome them through His power, grace, and mercy in our lives.

3 James Weldon Johnson, *God's Trombones: Seven Negro Sermons in Verse* (New York: Penguin Books, reprint 1990), p. 21, "The Prodigal Son."

4 "...Without any support whatever from himself, he [Jacob] hangs upon the conqueror, and in that condition learns by experience the practice of sole reliance on one mightier than himself. This is the turning point in this strange drama. Henceforth Jacob now feels himself strong, not in himself, but in the Lord, and in the power of his might." *Barnes' Notes*, by Albert Barnes, D.D., Electronic Database (Biblesoft, 1997), s.v. "Genesis 32:1-32, Verses 23-32."

5 "...The reason...is...he [the angel] would not any longer detain Jacob, who had business to do, a journey to go, a family to look after, which, especially in this critical juncture, called for his attendance. Note, Every thing is beautiful in its season; even the business of religion, and the comforts of communion with God, must sometimes give way to the necessary affairs of this life...." *Matthew Henry's Commentary*, s.v. "Genesis 32:24-32, Jacob wrestles with an angel."

6 "...since Jacob continued wrestling all night, and was not blessed until 'the breaking of the day,' so God frequently does not answer the prayers of His people until the last moment—until, by the very delay—strengthening the spirit of prayer, and by the continued exercise of it—their hearts are brought into such a state of submission and of faith, that they become fit recipients of the blessing." *Jamieson, Fausset and Brown Commentary*, Electronic Database (Biblesoft, 1997), s.v. "Genesis 32:24-30, Verse 26."

7 Strong, "Hebrew and Chaldee Dictionary," p. 51, entry #3290, s.v. "Jacob," Genesis 32:27.

8 See Genesis 25:29-34.

9 See Revelation 1:6.

10 2 Corinthians 12:9.

Chapter 7

[1] Arthur Pink, pp. 341-408.

[2] Genesis 45:5-7.

[3] 1 John 1:7.

[4] 1 Corinthians 12:1-11; Galatians 5:22.

[5] Philippians 4:19.

Chapter 8

[1] This chapter contains the author's paraphrased narrative of the story of Isaiah and the aftermath of the death of King Uzziah. It is based on Isaiah 6.

[2] Based on a definition from Briggs and Gesenius, *The KJV Old Testament Hebrew Lexicon Brown*, "Hebrew Lexicon entry for Y@sha`yah," entry #3470, s.v. "Isaiah," available from <http://www.biblestudytools.net/Lexicons>.

[3] *Keil & Delitzsch Commentary on the Old Testament: New Updated Edition* (Hendrickson Publishers, Inc.: Electronic Database, 1996), s.v. "Isaiah 6:1." Used by permission. All rights reserved.

[4] Briggs and Gesenius, "Hebrew Lexicon entry for Kabowd," entry #3519, s.v. "glory," available from <http://www.biblestudytools.net/Lexicons>.

[5] Isaiah 7:14.

[6] Isaiah 9:7.

[7] Romans 5:8.

[8] Isaiah 9:6 AMP.

[9] The power of God had come upon them in that service in the same way we saw earlier that Isaiah fell to his knees when he felt the power of God on him as he came into God's Presence in the temple.

[10] Isaiah 49:15.

[11] Jeremy and Connie Sinnott, "Healing the Heart to Worship Him" from *Spread the Fire Magazine* (Volume 6, Issue 5, copyright © 2000; revised August 15, 2002). Available from <http://www.tacf.org/stf/6-5/feature4.html>.

[12] Based on a definition from Unger, s.v. "JOY." Zephaniah 3:17.

[13] Matthew 6:9.

[14] Steve Beard, ed., *The Good News Magazine,* a publication of the United Church of God, an International Association, "Sinners in the Hands of a Singing God," article available from <http://www.thunder-struck.org/holysmoke/1999-Singing%20GOD.htm>.

Chapter 9

[1] This chapter contains the author's paraphrased narrative of the story of the woman with the issue of blood, which is found in three of the Gospels: Matthew 9:20-22, Mark 5:25-34, and Luke 8:43-48.

Chapter 10

[1] John 14:8.

[2] John 14:9.

[3] Job 19:25,27.

[4] Isaiah 9:6.

[5] John 8:11.

[6] John 14:9.

[7] Matthew 7:11.

[8] Ernest Hemingway, "The Capital of the World" from *The Complete Short Stories of Ernest Hemingway* (New York: Simon & Schuster, 1987), p. 29.

Chapter 11

[1] Based on information from *The Handbook of Texas Online,* which is a joint project of The General Libraries at the University of Texas at Austin and the Texas State Historical Association. Available from <http://www.tsha.utexas.edu/handbook/online/index.new.html>.

[2] Based on information from a survey conducted in August 2002 by LegalZoom.com, Inc., a legal information Web site founded by attorneys from around the country. Results were taken from parents with minor children. Available from <http://news.findlaw.com/prnewswire/20020828/28aug2002042239.html>.

[3] John 16:7 KJV.

[4] Based on definitions from Vine, p. 207, s.v. "COMFORT, COMFORTER, COMFORTLESS, A. Nouns, 1. PARAKLESIS."

[5] Ibid, s.v. "5. PARAKLETOS," p. 208.

[6] See Deuteronomy 33:27.

[7] See Psalm 121:3,4.

[8] John 3:16.

[9] Hebrews 13:5.

[10] Psalm 23:4.

[11] See John 6:63.

[12] See 2 Corinthians 5:21; 1 Corinthians 1:24.

[13] See Ephesians 6:14.

[14] See Exodus 13:21.

[15] See Romans 8:16,17.

[16] Javaka Steptoe, *In Daddy's Arms I Am Tall: African Americans Celebrating Fathers* (New York: Lee & Low Books Inc., 1997), first entry.

Chapter 12

[1] Doug Banister, *Sacred Quest: Discovering Spiritual Intimacy with God* (Grand Rapids: Zondervan Publishing House, 2001), pp. 56,57.

[2] Luke 2:42-49.

[3] Matthew 3:17.

[4] Luke 11:1.

[5] See John 5:19; 12:50; 14:10.

[6] Mark 14:36.

[7] Matthew 26:53.

[8] Luke 23:34 KJV.

[9] Luke 23:46 KJV.

[10] See Acts 1:4.

[11] At the time we ask Jesus to be our Lord and Savior and receive Him in our heart, we receive the Holy Spirit. But we can receive the fullness of the Holy Spirit by asking God to fill us completely with His Spirit, which empowers and enables us to live the Christian life. (See Acts 1:8; 10:44,45.)

[12] See Psalm 139:1-4,17,18.

[13] See James 5:20.

[14] See Isaiah 40:11 NLT.

[15] See 1 Corinthians 6:20; 1 Peter 1:18,19.

[16] Brennan Manning, *Abba's Child: The Cry of the Heart for Intimate Belonging* (Colorado Springs: NavPress, 1994).

Chapter 13

[1] Based on research from the National Runaway Switchboard, available from <http://www.nrscrisisline.org>. The NRS services are provided in part through funding from the Washington D.C.-based Family and Youth Services Bureau in the Administration for Children and Families, US Department of Health and Human Services.

[2] *Guinness World Records,* s.v. "bees," available from <http://www.guinnessworldrecords.com>.

[3] Psalm 142:4.

[4] Strong, "Greek Dictionary of the New Testament," p. 43, entry #2853, s.v. "joined," Luke 15:15.

[5] Based on a translation from Fritz Reinecker and Cleon Rogers III, *Linguistic Key to the Greek New Testament.* Translation from the German (Grand Rapids: Regency Reference Library, 1976), p. 187, s.v. "Luke 15:26."

[6] Helmut Thielicke, *Life Can Begin Again: Sermons on the Sermon on the Mount* (Philadelphia: Fortress Press, 1963), p. 112.

[7] Nathan E. Han, AZ, compiler, *Parsing Guide to the Greek New Testament* (Scottsdale, Pennsylvania: Herald Press, 1971) entry "Luke 15:20."

[8] "The ring was at a very ancient date a symbol of authority and dignity...." Unger, s.v. "RING."

[9] Isaiah 52:7; Romans 10:15.

[10] Charles H. Spurgeon, "Many Kisses for Returning Sinners, or Prodigal Love for the Prodigal Son," sermon #2236, preached December, 1891, available from the archives in <http://www.spurgeon.org/sermons/2236.htm>.

Chapter 14

[1] This chapter contains the author's paraphrased narrative of the story of Peter—how he denied the Lord three times and the aftermath of that denial—what happened to Peter after that night. It is found in all four of the Gospels, including Matthew 26 and 27; Mark 14 and 16; Luke 22 and 24; John 13:38, and John 18, 20, and 21.

Chapter 15

[1] 1 Corinthians 12:27.

[2] See 2 Timothy 2:15 KJV.

[3] Matthew 16:18 KJV.

[4] Acts 10:38.

[5] See Psalm 133:1; Ephesians 4:1,3,13.

[6] See 1 Corinthians 12:1,4,8-10; Ephesians 4:7,8.

Chapter 16

[1] Ecclesiastes 3:11.

[2] See John 3:3.

[3] See Romans 6:4-6; 8:23.

[4] Strong, "Hebrew and Chaldee Dictionary," p. 85, entry #5703, s.v. "everlasting," Isaiah 9:6.

[5] 2 Corinthians 5:8.

[6] Mark 12:29 KJV.

[7] Revelation 22:4.

[8] "My Savior First of All," words by Fanny Crosby, music by John R. Sweney, 1894; available from <http://www.cyberhymnal.org>.

[9] See 1 Corinthians 15:52-54.

[10] Vine, "Vol. IV. Set-Z," p. 94, s.v. "SUPPLY, A. Verbs, 1. CHOREGEO; 2. EPICHOREGEO."

[11] Strong, "Greek Dictionary of the New Testament," p. 32, entry #2023, s.v. "shall be ministered," 2 Peter 1:11.

[12] See Galatians 5:5.

[13] 2 Corinthians 5:8.

Prayer of Salvation

God loves you—no matter who you are, no matter what your past. God loves you so much that He gave His one and only begotten Son for you. The Bible tells us that "...whoever believes in him shall not perish but have eternal life" (John 3:16 NIV). Jesus laid down His life and rose again so that we could spend eternity with Him in heaven and experience His absolute best on earth. If you would like to receive Jesus into your life, say the following prayer out loud and mean it from your heart.

Heavenly Father, I come to You admitting that I am a sinner. Right now, I choose to turn away from sin, and I ask You to cleanse me of all unrighteousness. I believe that Your Son, Jesus, died on the cross to take away my sins. I also believe that He rose again from the dead so that I might be forgiven of my sins and made righteous through faith in Him. I call upon the name of Jesus Christ to be the Savior and Lord of my life. Jesus, I choose to follow You and ask that You fill me with the power of the Holy Spirit. I declare that right now I am a child of God. I am free from sin and full of the righteousness of God. I am saved in Jesus' name. Amen.

If you prayed this prayer to receive Jesus Christ as your Savior for the first time, please contact us on the web at www.harrisonhouse.com to receive a free book.

Or you may write to us at
Harrison House
P.O. Box 35035
Tulsa, Oklahoma 74153

About the Author

In 1979, Ron Phillips was called as pastor of Central Baptist Church located in the Chattanooga, Tennessee, area, where he serves today. Under his ministry this Southern Baptist church has experienced the birth and growth of many ministries, broken records in church giving and attendance, and completed several building projects. But more importantly, the church has exploded into new realms of renewal and spiritual awakening.

While joy seems to flow from every aspect of Pastor Phillips' ministry today, God had to take him through a painful growing process. Over his years of service, Pastor Phillips served on many boards and committees. Having earned a bachelor's degree from Samford University in Birmingham, Alabama, as well as a Masters of Divinity and a Doctorate of Ministry from New Orleans Baptist Theological Seminary, his successes were many. But in 1989 he felt in his spirit that the joy in serving had left him.

He was burned out in ministry and ready to resign when he had an encounter with the Holy Spirit that changed his life forever. The voice of God in his heart literally interrupted his sleep and spoke peace and transformation to his soul. This dynamic encounter started the fires of rebirth that soon spread to the church and every aspect of ministry. Pastor Phillips began to introduce the things of the Spirit that the Lord was teaching him, and the flames of awakening began to heat up the spiritual temperature of the members and spread outward, crossing denominational lines.

With Pastor Phillips' new anointing came a deeper passion to reach across America and eventually around the world with the powerful message of Christ and the power of the Holy Spirit. He is a sought-after conference and crusade speaker, taking engagements as far away as Iceland and Nigeria, Africa.

The weekly television broadcast "The Central Message," featuring Dr. Phillips' preaching ministry, is seen all around the world. In addition, he hosts the daily 15-minute radio program "CenterPoint" on stations across the nation and throughout the world via the Internet.

Along with demand for the broadcast ministry has grown the need for Pastor Phillips' teaching to be put into print. He is the author of twelve books and a variety of articles and booklets, including *Vanquishing the Enemy, Awakened by the Spirit,* and *Made Kindred by the Spirit.*

Serving beside him is his wife, Paulette, a gifted, sought-after speaker herself, who leads several classes at Central Baptist Church and travels to speak at conference and banquet events around the country. Ron and Paulette are the parents of three grown children who reside in the Chattanooga, Tennessee area. Ron and Paulette reside in Hixson, Tennessee.

In his unceasing commitment to preach the Word of God, Ron Phillips has enlarged his vision for souls throughout his years of ministry. Future growth plans for his church and ministry indicate that this vision will continue to increase in scope.

To contact Ron Phillips write:

Central Baptist Church
5208 Hixson Pike
Hixson, TN 37343
423-877-6462

www.ronphillips.org

*Please include your prayer requests
and comments when you write.*

Other Books by Dr. Ron Phillips

Malachi: Hope at the End of an Age

Hebrews: Finding the Better Way

Made Kindred by the Spirit

Awakened by the Spirit:
Reclaiming the Forgotten Gift of God

The Spirit of Christmas (contributor)

Vanquishing the Enemy:
Triumphant in the Battles of Life

Home Improvement:
A Maintenance & Repair Manual for Families

Isaiah: Light for Days of Darkness

Song of Solomon: Invitation To Intimacy

The Church Transformed To Triumph (2 Corinthians)

Signs of Life (John)

The Royal Law of Royal Giving (James)

Additional copies of this book
are available from your local bookstore.

If this book has been a blessing to you
or if you would like to see more of the
Harrison House product line,
please visit us on our website at
www.harrisonhouse.com

Harrison House
Tulsa, Oklahoma 74153

The Harrison House Vision

Proclaiming the truth and the power

Of the Gospel of Jesus Christ

With excellence;

Challenging Christians to

Live victoriously,

Grow spiritually,

Know God intimately.